Divorce Buddy System™

The Real Secret to a Reasonable Divorce

J. Richard Kulerski, J.D.

AuthorHouse™
1663 Liberty Drive, Suite 200
Bloomington, IN 47403
www.authorhouse.com
Phone: 1-800-839-8640

© *2008 J. Richard Kulerski, J.D.. All rights reserved.*

No part of this book may be used or reproduced by any means – graphic, electronic or mechanical, including photocopying, recording, taping or by any information storage retrieval system – without the written permission of the author, except in the case of brief quotations embodied in critical articles and reviews.

First published by AuthorHouse 10/10/2008

ISBN: 978-1-4343-3752-8 (sc)
ISBN: 978-1-4343-3753-5 (e)
ISBN: 978-1-4343-3751-1 (hc)

Printed in the United States of America
Bloomington, Indiana

This book is printed on acid-free paper.

A Quick Note

Divorce Buddy System^{TM} is about a different way to divorce. It is aimed at helping reasonable people get a reasonable divorce without the legal system adding to their pain or expense.

It reveals exactly what the parties can say and do to join forces to beat the high cost and frustration of going to court.

Scuba divers use what they call the buddy system whenever they make a dive. This means they swim in pairs and stay together at all times.

The purpose is safety. If one diver runs into trouble (e.g., runs out of air, gets stuck in a confined area, etc.), the other diver is there to help out.

And this is how I would ask you to view the buddy system in divorce. Instead of two divers joining forces for their common good, it is two spouses joining forces to control the length, pain and expense of their divorce.

Divorce Buddy System represents the future spirit of divorce.

Feel free to skip around. The book is designed so you can read it in any order you choose. It is quick and easy reading, and there is no homework, drills or exercises.

Table of Contents

Opening Statement	xi
They Don't Give Us Divorce Lessons	xii
Our Plan for Your Divorce	xii

SECTION I – Your Divorce – What You Are Up Against

Chapter 1 – We Can Work It Out	3
Why Can't We Just Settle the Divorce Ourselves?	4
An X-Ray of the Problem	6
Just the Facts, Ma'am	8
We've Been Using the Wrong Fork	8
Chapter 2 – Who Stole the Cow?	11
Lead Us Not Into Litigation	12
The Brutal Truth	13
The Way We War	14
Call Your First Witness	14

SECTION II – The New Divorce – Yes, You Can Beat the System

Chapter 3 – Divorce Court Is No Place for a Divorce	19
Habeas Court-less	20
Our Bottle of Nitroglycerin	22
What the World Needs Now	22
Chapter 4 – The Key to the Buddy System – The Eleventh Commandment	25
The Three Major Things	27
A Little Change Will Do You Good	28
Silent Might	30
Never Put Your Mouth Where Your Money Is	31

SECTION III – *How* You Will Get through Your Divorce in One Peace

Chapter 5 – Shake Hands & Come Out Negotiating	**35**
Let's Make a Deal	36
Irritable Spouse Syndrome	36
Define a "Reasonable" Spouse	37
Does It Really Take Two to Tangle?	38
Don't Cut Off Your Nose to Spite Your Face	38
Chapter 6 – The Courthouse Door	**41**
If You Build It, They Will Calm	41
Make Up Your Own House Rules	44
Take the Pulse	47
Chapter 7 – The Blinding Power of Perspectives	**49**
Who Gets a Raw Deal – Men or Women?	50
Why Should I Care What My Spouse Thinks?	50
Are There Really Two Sides to Every Story?	51
The Boulder	52
Getting Around the Boulder	52
Heart and Soul	53
Chapter 8 – Emotions: Disturbing the Peace	**55**
Jack of All Tirades	55
Blamer v. Blamer	56
Cat Should Get Your Tongue	57
The Six Miracle Words	58
Minimum Rage	59
Post-Romantic Stress	61
Full Court Stress	61
The Weary Traveler	62
Peace by Peace	63
The Peace Academy	64
Chapter 9 – Language & Listening: Now Ear This	**67**
As the Word Turns	67
Non-Friction Diction	68

He Said, She Said	69
The Speakers of the House – Getting Your Spouse to Open Up	69
He Hears Me, She Hears Me Not	71
I'm All Ears	72
Knock Three Times	73
Friendly Persuasion	74
Hear-Say	77
An Ear for an Ear	78
Hearing Aids	78

Chapter 10 – The Obstacle Course – Nine Invisible Hurdles & How To Jump Them — 83

One Spouse Wants a Divorce, One Doesn't	83
Take This Deal and Love It	85
You Won't Find Feelings on a Spreadsheet	87
You Started It	89
Divorce Papers Are Scary	91
You Can't Spend a Pound of Flesh	92
Incoming! Incoming!	93
Cogito, Ergo Sue 'em	95
Trust or Consequences	97

Chapter 11 – What to Do When – Eleven Specific Situations & Curveballs — 99

1: Who Should Make the First Offer?	99
2: When Your Spouse Pushes for a Ball Park Number (Or, What's Behind Curtain #3?)	102
3: Leave Haggling to the Hagglers	102
4: Does the First One to Speak Always Lose?	103
5: Or Else What? When Your Spouse Gives an Ultimatum	103
6: When Your Spouse Pushes for an Answer	104
7: Is That a Threat?	105
8: When Your Spouse Heads for the Door	105
9: Speaking to the Devil – Negotiation Bullies	106
10: Negotiating via E-mail and Telephone	107
11: Your Lawyer's Place or Mine?	108

Chapter 12 – Where Do I Sign? ... 111
The Golden Bridge ... 111
True Concessions ... 112
Nibbling ... 113
No One Likes a Lousy Winner ... 114

Conclusion – Your Divorce Masterpeace ... 115
You Really Didn't Want Blood, Did You? ... 116
Goodbye, Divorce Wars…Hello, Dotted Line ... 117

Index ... 119

Opening Statement

I want what is best for my kids.
I only want what is fair.
I don't want to hurt my spouse.
I want to avoid a court battle and all the legendary pandemonium.
I don't want the divorce to drag on forever.
I definitely don't want it to cost an arm and a leg.

Do these sound familiar? I'm betting they do.

Of course you don't "want" a divorce, but here you are, confronting one. And you are saying the six universal things that I have heard most new clients say throughout all of my 40-plus years as a practicing divorce lawyer.

While some parties do seek vengeance and retribution during divorce, I find that most people do not fundamentally desire the additional pain and expense of fighting it out in court. Once they get over the shock of the divorce, their preference is generally to get on with their lives as quickly and as smoothly as possible.

At least, that's what they say, and I believe most spouses mean it. I know I surely did. (More about those who don't in Chapter 5)

I've written *Divorce Buddy System* for the parties who really mean it.

So, how *do* you get through your divorce with minimum pain and expense?

For most of us, the answer lies in how we behave during the divorce.

They Don't Give Us Divorce Lessons

A sensible way to learn something is by accepting guidance from someone who already knows it. When we want to learn how to knit, drive, play the piano or use karate, we find an expert and take lessons. Need tax help? We talk to a CPA.

We have resources for every imaginable endeavor, from hobbies to finances to sports. Community colleges offer parenting classes to prospective parents; there are even lactation experts to teach mothers how to breast-feed their babies.

Yet, society offers us very little insight into what we can do to keep our divorces from becoming train wrecks. This is particularly startling when we consider that more than half of all marriages end in divorce.

It seems that we're always being told how to behave during marriage, but no one ever tells us how to behave during divorce.

Our Plan for Your Divorce

And this brings us to the point of *Divorce Buddy System*.

The buddy system in divorce is another way of saying "If you can't beat 'em, join 'em." And, you're better off joining them because you are doomed if you don't. (The Brutal Truth, Chapter 2)

This book shows you exactly what to say and do (and not say and do) to join forces with your soon-to-be ex so the two of you can beat the legal system, instead the other way around.

We'll explain the missing link – the one thing that could have saved our predecessors from countless unnecessary divorce wars (and the answer was always right under our nose) – along with the why's and how's of our present divorce legal system.

We'll next jump into the main course – an eye-opening exploration of the fundamentals of the buddy approach and how they help you influence your spouse and your monetary settlement.

Then we'll get specific about how to use this eye-opening information effectively. I'll share precise, step-by-step instructions for making your divorce more tolerable, without costing you that proverbial arm and leg.

The legal process does not always make this easy (more on this in Section I), but you will be able to sidestep the trouble and keep your divorce on time and on budget.

You will also learn how to deal with the many invisible obstacles and curveballs that are likely to come your way.

Finally, we'll wrap it all up with some last words of advice and encouragement.

Our divorce rate indicates that we are not doing very well staying married. And judging by the length, expense, drama, and trauma of the average divorce, it looks like we, as a nation, aren't much better at becoming unmarried.

Marriage is difficult by nature, but divorce isn't. *Getting divorced is mostly difficult by choice.* The trick is to not get in our own way.

So, if you are among those seeking a divorce who –

- want what is best for the kids
- only want what is fair
- are not out to hurt your spouse
- want to avoid a court battle and all the legendary pandemonium
- don't want the divorce to take forever; and
- definitely don't want it to cost an arm and a leg

– then you are holding in your hand a guide with all you need to know about containing the fury, pain, and cost of your divorce.

SECTION I

Your Divorce – What You Are Up Against

Chapter 1
We Can Work It Out

Divorce. The word has been said out loud.

I'm not referring to minor marital spats in which the D word is often thrown around frivolously. I am speaking of the conversations which occur when both partners realize that, this time, the talk of divorce is probably more than just talk.

At this early juncture, we are able to focus on only the emotional aspect of the breakup. We need some time to get past the initial shock before we can turn to any of the legal or financial ramifications.

Our brain brings us along slowly and protects us from experiencing the full impact of both aspects simultaneously. It creates a coping tool which allows us to process these events without hitting "tilt." We induce our own form of anesthesia; we shoot up with denial.

And so we buy into our spouse's assurances that he or she plans on being "fair." (If you know of someone whose partner didn't start out promising to be fair, contact "Ripley's Believe It or Not" at once.) We are hurting and we need to believe that our spouse is not planning on adding to our hurt. The promise of fairness relieves some of the pain and confirms our ability to judge human nature.

It makes it easier to tell our family and friends about the divorce. Plus, we are not in a hurry to face the possibility that they may have been right about our marriage partner all along. The promise to be fair buys us some time before we have to deal with the possibility of hearing *I told you so.*

The news is not as devastating to our family when the soon-to-be ex promises to be fair.

Our "Mr. or Mrs. Nice Guy" anesthesia typically wears off at the same time our better half announces that "fair" means they should get our half, too.

Why Can't We Just Settle the Divorce Ourselves?

Many of us try to keep our divorces from becoming difficult, but the reality is that most of us will not be able to do so. This is because we suffer from a common problem, which is as old as divorce itself. We seem to be unaware of its existence despite the fact that it continues to claim more victims every day. We know something is to blame for turning our divorce into a nightmare, but it never occurs to us that this is the culprit.

Here it is – the problem that we don't know is a problem:

We really don't know how to discuss a divorce settlement with our spouse. We think we do, but we don't.

For starters, we truly fail to comprehend how much and how quickly things change once a divorce gets underway.

On a purely intellectual level, we recognize that it should now be harder for us to influence our partner's thinking. However, once we are actually feeling the reality of our divorce, this intellectual insight flies right over our heads. As far as we're concerned, it's marriage as usual, and our spouse is just as susceptible to our reasoning and charm as ever before. We delude ourselves into believing that we can still influence their thinking. After all, we shared a life with this person and, if we can't convince them to see things correctly, who can?

Our next misstep is that we rely on the same communication skills we used during the marriage – the only ones we have to work with – to be of assistance to us during the divorce. But talk about delusion. Our inability to communicate effectively with one another is probably why we are getting divorced in the first place. If we couldn't get through to them before, it is nuts to think we can get through to them now. It's no wonder we have divorce wars.

To make things worse, we often ignore the fact that our fighting may have been going on for years, perhaps since the very start. (Some of us are so cantankerous we probably started fighting with our spouse before we even met.) Yet we somehow find a way to believe that our inability to communicate effectively with our partner will get the job done for us. When it doesn't? Well, it must be the legal system's fault.

So, we naïvely assume that our soon-to-be-ex will see the numbers and facts as *we* do, and then accept the deal *we* want them to accept. We don't realize it at the time, but this is about as doable as herding cats or nailing jelly to a wall.

In other words, this just doesn't happen, despite the fact that we are universally optimistic about pulling it off. We instinctively suppress anything that might undermine our belief that our spouse will go along with our plan. We ignore their stated dislike of us, our long-standing inability to communicate with one another, and even the Buttinsky Factor. Yes, it barely fazes us that our partner is marching to orders received from friends and family who probably dislike us even more than the soon-to-be ex does.

None of this shakes our confidence. We put on our denial blinders and set out to get our way. And we really think we will.

Boy, are we wrong. It's like whispering into a jet engine.

Here's why. We don't have a clue about what works and what doesn't. And this isn't our fault. Divorce puts us at our worst at a time in our life when we must be at our best, and no one ever told us about the "be at our best" part. We think we still have the freedom to say what's on our mind, and we do not.

No one ever told us to check our guns at the door.

Divorce is new territory. It puts into play emotions, perspectives, and other phenomena that require special handling. Our common sense, verbal skills, and general savvy (which may serve us well in other parts of our life) do not prepare us for these conversations. It's too easy to get caught off guard by forces we don't comprehend and are not prepared to handle.

Think of all the people you know who started out expecting a smooth and friendly divorce, and, instead, wound up wondering what hit them.

And, in my opinion, those who are able to settle on their own are the exception. The rest of us are usually not this lucky.

An X-Ray of the Problem

So, the basic problem is that we really don't know how to discuss a divorce settlement with our partner. But what *specifically* makes our spousal divorce settlement conversations difficult?

There are many reasons for this, and we'll cover them all. I think our difficulty starts with our general naïveté, unreceptive attitude, and defensive posture. They combine to form a broad template of negativity upon which the blank spaces are filled in with specific destructive factors (Chapters 7 through 9) that apply to our individual divorce.

The naïveté we've already discussed, but what about attitude and defensiveness? Let's talk about these now.

To help illustrate, please allow me to ask you a question:

Do you feel divorcing parties are inclined to fib about their income or assets?

I believe our adversarial culture plants a distrusting bias in our mind. It tells us that divorcing spouses are out for all they can get and are not above getting cute when it comes to money.

Generations of youngsters have overheard whispers of how Aunt So-and-So got the short end of the stick in her divorce or about how "cool" it is to slip one past the other party. Legend perpetually speaks of the proverbial unsuspecting spouse who now wishes that he or she "had known better."

The message passed on to us is that society is not altogether offended by this behavior. While it is not condoned, the behavior certainly seems to be expected. This alone is sufficient to put us on heightened alert and cause us to arrive at the bargaining table with an in-your-face attitude of negativity and distrust. It doesn't take much more than this to put both parties on the defensive right from the start.

And when we are in a defensive mode, we are anything but receptive. It's not easy to sell something to a person who is already poised to pounce on the first word they don't agree with. Heaven forbid if one of us should ask for something that the other feels entitled to.

Defensive people are edgy, difficult to please, and are not at all inclined to entertain someone else's settlement wishes. Even if this resistant demeanor doesn't catapult us into the next world war, it usually ends our willingness to hear our spouse's side of the story.

And make no mistake about it: these conversations are big. They are when every word counts and when sensible divorces are made and broken. There are no dress rehearsals; if we say it, we're stuck with it.

Unfortunately, without specific instruction to the contrary or a tremendous amount of good fortune, we are more likely than not to react with our own attitude toward our spouse's attitude, say the wrong thing, and shut down our settlement hopes. As a result, most of our who-should-get-what-in-the-divorce conversations are doomed from the start.

Our naiveté really hits home when our partner says no to our settlement proposal. Their *no* brings an end to our fantasy world and makes us look reality in the eye. Since we know they are wrong and we are right, we become upset and react with more attitude; and then so do they.

Is upsetting someone just before asking them to give or accept something that they are unwilling to give or accept a sensible way to begin negotiating? Of course it isn't. However, this has been our norm, so there should be little wonder that so many of our divorces turn into horror stories.

So here we are – naïve, unreceptive, and defensive – facing both the emotional and legal ramifications of the end of our marriage, and putting all our eggs in the basket of belief that we will be able to talk sense with our soon-to-be ex's.

In such an environment, even partners whose hearts are in the right place can unwittingly trigger hostility without ever realizing what they did to cause it. This is why most homemade settlement attempts fall apart in the early stages.

As countless reasonable people who have already endured the divorce process will agree, being reasonable and wanting a less painful, less expensive divorce is simply not enough to guarantee a smooth settlement. Among the reasons for this are some cold facts that they never told us about.

Just the Facts, Ma'am
>**FACT:** The vast majority of divorcing spouses do not want their cases to take a long time or cost a lot of money.
>
>**FACT:** You can save time and money if you can settle your case quickly and out of court.
>
>**FACT:** In order to settle quickly and out of court, you must be able to get your spouse to say yes to a settlement agreement.
>
>**FACT:** Your spouse will say yes only if it benefits them to do so.
>
>**FACT:** You will not be able to explain those benefits because your spouse will not listen to reason.
>
>**FACT:** Your spouse will not listen to reason because we do not know how to give them a reason to listen.

Sound like mumbo jumbo? Maybe. But this mumbo jumbo happens to hold the solution to the oldest and most expensive mystery in divorce.

It explains why it is so hard for divorcing partners to persuade each other to agree to a settlement.

We've Been Using the Wrong Fork
We have been going about divorce all wrong. If the world is our oyster, we have been using the wrong fork. We thought we could get through to our spouse by explaining the reasonableness of *our* position. This does not work; in fact, a century of divorce wars proves it does not work. No, we get through to our spouse by listening to the reasonableness of *their* position.

We listen and we continue to listen. We listen until their stance begins to soften and their thinking becomes moldable. We don't argue with them; we just listen until they discover (as reasonable people do) that compromise doesn't mean losing. It just means they have discovered another acceptable solution.

Our partner's mind is locked during divorce and can be opened only from the inside. So, if we hope to gain entry and disengage their resistance, our best bet is to stop talking and start listening. Their deadbolts will remain in place until we've heard every last word they have to say.

Don't believe it? Then please ask yourself what it would take for your spouse to get you to change *your* mind.

Would you ever really consider compromising if all that your partner did was to argue in favor of their position?

Or, would you be more inclined to loosen up if they showed a genuine willingness to understand your side, too?

So, without realizing the futility of it all, we've spent the past century pleading our cases to a brick wall. What we really needed to keep things (or our spouse) on track was someone to guide us around the wall.

Instead, we turned to the legal system for assistance. It was the only game in town, and it wasn't enough.

The next chapter explains why we cannot get the help we need from the legal system. Don't concern yourself with this because, in just a few hours, the new you will have the finesse of a negotiation locksmith.

Chapter 2
Who Stole the Cow?

Once upon a time, allegedly centuries ago, a villager was accused of stealing another villager's cow. The accused villager denied all guilt. This disagreement gave birth to our first civil (as opposed to criminal) trial.

The objective was to have an impartial party determine who, if anyone, owed what, if anything, to whom – in other words, to settle the dispute once and for all. Strict rules were quickly put in place to keep order. Witnesses were sworn to tell the truth or be punished. There could be no middle ground. Either the accused took the cow or he didn't. Only one party would win and the other would lose.

That's the essence of what it means to be adversarial: winner take all.

> There was never a good war or a bad peace.
> —*Benjamin Franklin (1706-1790)*

During the centuries since that poor cow was stolen, the villager dispute/resolution model evolved into the civil court system we have today. When divorce became part of our law, the divorce courts were made a part of the civil court system. Since that system is adversarial, so are divorce courts.

In many jurisdictions, the judge who hears your divorce case today may be sitting in the very same courtroom tomorrow presiding over a death penalty or airline crash case. The subject matter of the cases may vary, but the decorum, procedures, and rules of evidence are the same. And they are all based on the adversarial system.

Here's what my thesaurus associates with the word *adversarial*: hostile, antagonistic, conflicting, opposing, nail-biting, nerve-racking, scary, intimidating, menacing, frightening, chilling, macabre, terrifying, bloodcurdling.

Why adversarial and not something more mellow? After all, these are family matters, aren't they?

Because the Constitution prohibits taking someone's property without due process of law, and that means using the strict, unwavering standards that go hand in hand with the adversarial approach.

The mere involvement of the legal system often puts unintended trouble into play. Its very tradition, rigid culture, and formality can tense up the best of us. Its presence adds all sorts of apprehension and anxiety to an already combustible mix. This happens even when the divorce papers do not place blame on either party.

No wonder we behave the way we do when divorce enters our life. We are acting according to the combative beliefs of years gone by, which, unfortunately, still hold sway.

Lead Us Not Into Litigation

Litigation is a lawsuit in progress. If we are in a legal proceeding, we are in litigation. It includes the entire court process, from the filing of the case until the judge reaches a decision.

Those who enter the divorce legal system want something their spouse will not agree to give. The role of the court is to conduct a trial to determine which partner will get their way.

While the court encourages settlement, it must act on the assumption that a trial will be necessary. This requires the parties to gear up for the trial, routinely spending months (and lots of dollars) preparing for something that, statistically, isn't going to happen. (It is commonly believed by divorce lawyers and judges that over 90 percent of all divorce cases settle before trial, with many settling on the very eve of trial.)

Divorcing spouses are not in pleasant spirits when they arrive in the legal system, and things get progressively worse as the litigation process unfolds. Each party blames the other for putting them in a marital breakup, which they feel they did not cause and certainly do not deserve. They attribute the litigation to their partner's greed, stubbornness or general obstinacy. They are angry about being required to enter a forum they fear, while being accompanied by a member of a profession they have been warned not to trust.

And this is just the start.

Now, with a trial on the horizon, the parties enter into intense competition in which they must focus on winning. There is seldom any middle ground – at least none that either finds acceptable. One will win and one will lose.

Or so it seems.

The Brutal Truth

Quite simply, there are no winners in a divorce battle; everyone loses. Make no mistake about it. Here's why:

1. Our legal system cannot give us more than we have when we enter it.

2. No matter what we have when we enter the system, we will leave with less.

And this is *before* the lawyers get a dime.

These are ABSOLUTE TRUTHS. Divorcing spouses who opt to go all the way to trial deserve to know what is waiting for them at the finish line. They need to know that, in all likelihood, they are investing their time, money, and hopes on a mere illusion.

The outcome of a divorce trial can define only the extent of your loss. It cannot define victory because victory has never been in the cards.

> I was never ruined but twice: once when
> I lost a lawsuit and once when I won one.
> —*Voltaire*

The Way We War

Divorcing spouses usually see little reason to compromise. Each believes his or her position to be the correct one. So, why should the one who is right give any ground to the one who is wrong?

Participants in competition are not objective. As each day passes, they tend to become more driven and set in their thinking. Settlement is for those who may lose, and they plan on winning.

Besides, they do not wish to appear scared or weak, so they act tough and unyielding. If settlement is touched upon, they scoff with disrespect. Their posturing intensifies as they take turns shooting down each other's settlement overtures. In general, things escalate in the wrong direction.

Litigation reduces cases to black and white, and this is pure fantasy when it comes to divorce. It makes the parties think there is, indeed, a possibility of a happy ending.

Right. Ask around and see how many former divorce litigants you can find who were happy at the end of their cases. *Everyone* leaves the litigation process feeling frustrated, disillusioned, and poorer. It's like mental cruelty all over again.

Call Your First Witness

Spouses entering the divorce legal system for the first time mistakenly believe they will get to speak their minds in court. Finally someone will actually listen to what they've had to go through!

However, this rarely happens. In the first place, over nine out of every 10 divorcing spouses will reach a settlement before they ever get to speak to a judge.

More important, even those who actually do testify at trial do not get to say what they want to say. They are allowed to speak only when answering questions put to them by the lawyers, and the rules of evidence allow the lawyers to ask only what is legally relevant.

This rarely includes the injustices, the dishonesty, the betrayal, the adultery, the lies, the pain, the unfairness, and most of the other things that the parties think the judge should hear.

Instead, when deciding a case, the judge must stick to the relevant facts and the applicable law. The court is unable to consider the parties' underlying humanity, which is the very fulcrum upon which the parties base their sense of justice and entitlement.

Simply put, the law is the standard by which the court will judge your case. Your emotions, feelings, and pain do not count in a courtroom. The judge will not even learn of these things, because they are not admissible.

The judge's hands are often tied because the real boss in this context is the state legislature (the lawmakers) which tells the judge what he or she can or cannot do.

Judges determine what happens to real people in real-life situations. They have to look people in the eye and dispense what is often cookie-cutter justice. The lawmakers don't have to look anything in the eye but another cigar; they do not see the faces and tears of those most affected by the laws they write.

Judges do the best they can, under the circumstances, to achieve equity and fairness. They try to give every litigant fair consideration, but they can go only so far. In the final analysis, the judges must follow the law as it is and not as it (so often) should be.

Divorce is really about feelings, and the legal system isn't.

Litigation makes sense when there is a genuine need for it, but litigation in divorce is not just a legal mechanism. In other areas of law, litigation puts an end to a problem. Divorce does bring legal closure, but it often causes additional family problems. The emotional devastation caused by litigation can last for decades.

Litigation is an emotional vampire that sucks the spirit out of people.

And then there's the expense.

Few of us start out intending to spend large sums of money, but the cash outlay starts in acceptable, little steps, and then grows slowly until, finally, it gains momentum like a snowball rolling downhill.

Difficult divorces don't settle early. Serious settlement discussions usually don't take place until a case is pretty far along. By this time, most parties are disenchanted with the process and have spent more time, money, and energy than they ever thought possible. Many even accept the same settlement terms they rejected one or two years earlier.

Earlier, I recited a litany of things that divorcing spouses say *before* their case actually gets underway. The most common sentence divorce lawyers hear from clients *after* their case has started is this:

I just want it over with!

Parties who are new to the divorce legal system tend to focus on their partners' shortcomings or on the reason for the breakup. It doesn't take long before most become frustrated and disappointed with the legal system, and then shift their focus to its shortcomings. It's now a double-whammy – they are upset with their spouse and they are upset with the system they turned to for relief.

When we are hurting, we want help. And we have every right to expect it from the very mechanism society created for this purpose. However, to our dismay, what we expect is not what we get. The legal system isn't what we thought it would be. It doesn't run on time and it doesn't have the magic we want it to have.

Fortunately, there is a better way – the non-adversarial, non-confrontational buddy system way – that can

- create a sense of safety instead of fear
- facilitate your chances of an early settlement
- insulate your children from the dispute
- return control of the divorce to its owners, and
- require less healing time, by not inflicting new and unnecessary wounds on top of the existing ones

The buddy system approach offers what the adversarial approach does not now or ever could offer.

It addresses our basic human need to be understood.

SECTION II –

The New Divorce – Yes, You Can Beat the System

Chapter 3
Divorce Court Is No Place for a Divorce

Have you ever met anyone who thinks divorce litigation doesn't take too long and cost too much?

Do you know of even one person who, having gone through the divorce litigation process, would recommend it or do it again?

Yet, for the past century or so, and until just recently, this has been our only way to process a divorce case. Spouses unable to reach a settlement had no alternative but to wait in line in the court system for months – sometimes even for years – to get their opportunity to "slug it out" with one another.

Now, however, we have two additional methods of processing divorces: mediation and collaborative law.

These are two different dispute resolution models that share the same purpose and philosophy. Both provide trained professionals to help people in conflict to create their own resolution in an orderly, court-less, non-threatening, and sensible way. No one ever goes to court, except for the routine entry of papers that reflect what the parties agreed to.

Habeas Court-less

Mediation – the first "friendly" divorce settlement process to come along – provides in-meeting negotiation guidance to disputing parties who hope to avoid a court fight.

The parties meet with a neutral and impartial person (a mediator) who helps them communicate with one another in a level-headed way that disputants typically find difficult to achieve on their own. Mediators are trained to manage and defuse hostility and to keep negotiations headed in the right direction. They do not allow the participants' personalities or emotions to get in the way of settlement.

Mediators have no power to make decisions; their role is simply to help the parties create their own mutually acceptable resolution. In doing so, they use a variety of persuasion techniques that create and maintain a negotiation climate, which is conducive to settlement.

Most mediators are lawyers or licensed health professionals. Whatever their background or discipline, they typically undergo additional training in order to become proficient in mediation techniques. They must adhere to the standards of competency and ethics that are required by their state laws, local governing agencies or by the preferred practice group(s) with whom they are affiliated.

When mediation was first introduced, the community of divorce lawyers – myself included – said it didn't have enough teeth to be effective in divorce cases. We felt that it provided little incentive to disputants to accept terms they were opposed to, and that we needed the power of the court system to decide the terms for them.

We were wrong. It took some time, but mediation has flourished, and its success is now indisputable. It has gone on to help thousands of couples make it through the divorce process in a friendly, less costly and more dignified manner.

Collaborative law came along next and it rode on the coattails of mediation's success. This time I was an instant believer. It hit the ground running and continues to grow by leaps and bounds, truly exceeding all expectations.

Collaborative law is another form of assisted negotiation. Instead of a mediator being present, the parties have their own lawyers on the scene to guide the settlement discussions.

Collaborative lawyers don't make waves.

Collaborative lawyers provide legal services that are different from traditional legal services. They commit to helping the parties reach an out-of-court settlement and limit the scope of their employment to that of "settlement lawyers" only. The bulk of their legal work is performed privately at in-office settlement conferences with both attorneys and both parties in attendance.

The parties and their lawyers sign an agreement to work together toward reaching a settlement, and the lawyers agree they will not represent their client in court if a settlement is not reached.

Unlike mediators, collaborative lawyers are not neutral and impartial. They clearly represent the interests of their client only; but they do so in a non-threatening and settlement-friendly fashion.

Their clients enjoy the pleasantries of mediation, and they have the added comfort of knowing their lawyer is sitting right next to them.

Collaborative lawyers are required to retool their thinking and take special training in the dispute resolution intricacies and ethical application of the collaborative approach. Many are also trained mediators in their own right.

I often describe collaborative law as mediation with two opposing (but nevertheless helpful) mediators.

Despite these descriptions, this book is really not about mediation or collaborative law.

I mention them because they are based on exactly the same negotiation concept that the guts of this book are based on.

Mediation and collaborative law guide your actions *during* the actual mediation and collaborative law sessions, when the professionals are present. Their guidance ends when the session ends, similar to a dentist's work ending when the patient leaves the office.

The mediator and collaborative lawyers have you behave in sessions exactly as the buddy system has you behave when you are *outside* of the sessions, when the professionals are not there to pull you and your spouse apart.

Divorce Buddy System provides countless suggestions and tips for governing your out-of-session behavior; and they are all consistent with, if not identical to, the same in-session behavior that the mediator and collaborative lawyers require.

The buddy system also prepares you to act in your best interests during the weeks or months prior to your arrival in the divorce system. This helps to keep your settlement chances afloat until the professionals take over.

Our Bottle of Nitroglycerin

I like to use this example. Pretend that we carry an imaginary bottle of nitroglycerin with us. We are all prone to throw this explosive at our settlement chances whenever we are provoked.

When we enter mediation or collaborative law sessions, the mediator or our lawyer removes the nitro from our pocket without our ever knowing it is missing. Our spouse is so well regulated during the sessions that we don't ever have a need to reach for it.

But when the session ends and we are walking out the door, the nitroglycerin is secretly returned to our pocket, and we leave just as prone to destroying our settlement chances as we were when we walked in.

Divorce Buddy System makes it as though we never had the nitroglycerin to begin with. The principles of this book, and those of collaborative law and mediation, hold the future of divorce. A court-less future.

What the World Needs Now

Mediation, collaborative law, and the information on these pages represent the "court-less" approach. They are problem-solving techniques which are interest-based instead of power-based. Rather than rattling our sabers to intimidate our spouse into a settlement, we entice them to compromise by using their self-interests as leverage. We hook them with their desires and soften their resistance by using *their* wants to help us get what *we* want.

> **People are more inclined to be cooperative when they aren't dodging arrows.**

Divorce Buddy System™

Our traditional legal system represents the court (as opposed to the court-less) approach. It gives us a green light to be unpleasant toward our spouse and to vent our bitterness in any way we wish. Unfortunately, we usually do this right in our spouse's face, which is why the court way of doing things is a breeding ground for battlegrounds.

Here are some additional comparisons of the two approaches:

- **Court:** facts count more than feelings
- **Court-less:** feelings count more than facts

- **Court**: legal yardsticks determine the outcome
- **Court-less:** personal considerations help determine the outcome

- **Court:** the judge determines what is fair
- **Court-less:** the parties determine what is fair

- **Court:** what the judge says is law
- **Court-less:** what the spouses say is law

- **Court:** emotions do not count
- **Court-less:** emotions count a lot

- **Court:** good service to the marriage can be of little importance
- **Court-less:** good service to the marriage is always of great importance

- **Court:** the lawyers do the talking
- **Court-less:** the spouses do the talking

- **Court:** the spouses attack one another
- **Court-less:** the spouses join with one another and attack the problem

Need I say more?

Chapter 4
The Key to the Buddy System – The Eleventh Commandment

This is what makes the buddy system work. It is the link that has been missing since the day divorce was invented.

It is how you beat the system and keep your divorce from becoming unnecessarily painful and expensive. It boils down to this:

Act nicely toward your spouse, no matter what.
Act nicely even though they don't deserve it.
Act nicely even if it kills you.

You don't do it for them; you do it because it helps you get what you want. And, please don't brush this off as some talk show, touchy-feely gobbledygook. I admit "nice" is a wimpy word, and I probably should have substituted diplomatic, sensitive, pleasant, mature, etc., but I think "nice" gets the point across in a way that is harder to forget.

Now, as much as we would all like to control the pain and expense of our divorce, most people tend to draw the line at the "being nice" part. They find it downright unthinkable and rank it right up there with giving birth to an elephant.

The way I see it, if there is a better negotiation technique, the pros don't know about it. And, if they don't know about it, it doesn't exist.

Being nice during divorce flies in the face of what we know. We are taught to fight for our interests and to never show weakness in front of the opposition.

Thus, when our soon-to-be-ex is trying to stick it to us – whether in truth or just in our imagination – why should we be nice? Why should we care about their feelings, fears or concerns?

There is one power impact answer to these questions.

The fact is we do it to avoid a long, bad, ugly, divisive, and expensive divorce. We do it to save our dignity, mental stability, and physical health, and for the welfare of our children. Being nice does not mean being weak; it means being smart.

Sane divorce is about salesmanship, not war.

Anyone who has ever transacted business knows you must be nice to a customer if you wish to make a sale. Being nasty to a customer is bad business.

When you're in court, the judge is your customer – the one you must sell. Unless you are new to this planet, you will do everything you can to be nice to the judge.

When you want an out-of-court settlement, your spouse is the customer – the one you must sell to. It follows, therefore, that you should be nice to your spouse. If you want to make a deal, there are no buts.

Let's face it. If you don't want a court battle (and you don't use a gun or you don't hypnotize or lobotomize your partner), what other means do you have of motivating them to agree to a settlement they don't want to agree to?

This is where salesmanship comes in. It's all we have left – not to mention the coincidence of it also being the only thing that has ever been proven to work. In time, I'm hoping it will become the Eleventh Commandment.

Someone has to be nice first, or a calm and quick settlement is not going to happen.

The Three Major Things

So, exactly how would a person go about acting nicely (if, hypothetically, a person were to actually consider doing so)?

This is easy to explain. Acting nicely within the buddy system approach requires three major things:

1. Avoid aggravating your spouse.

2. Listen to what your spouse says and convince them you heard every word they said.

3. Know what to say and when to say it. Then say it nicely.

You'll be hearing more about these. Every negotiation insight and technique discussed in these pages is aimed at helping you accomplish at least one of the three. They are not jobs, tasks or must-dos; they are your new best friends.

If you are unsure whether something that you may say or do fits the description of acting nicely, keep the following scenario in mind. It may be too simplistic, but it does a pretty good job of portraying all you will ever need to know about the three major things.

1. Imagine that all your friends and entire family, and your spouse's friends and entire family, and all your neighbors, your employer, your customers . . . patients . . . clients . . . co-workers are watching and listening to your settlement conversation(s) on closed-circuit TV, and each of them will be given their own DVD version to watch and keep forever.

2. Even your children will get a copy when they come of age.

3. Then behave as you would want the world to see you behave.

If this is all you do, you are doing enough. It really is this simple.

A Little Change Will Do You Good

The old method of going straight to court is not working. It is no longer responsive to the public's needs. Divorce is more expensive, brutal, and unsatisfactory than ever before. The public is displeased and wants a change.

We must change our direction in order to change our destination. And the buddy system or nice approach is the change; it is our most sensible way to insure that our bad marriage is not followed by a bad divorce.

> If you want to make enemies, try to change something.
> —*Woodrow Wilson (1856-1924)*

The word "change" can have a positive or a negative connotation, depending on whether you are the one who wants it to happen. An aggrieved spouse is not likely to think highly of the kind of change I'm advocating – at least not upon first consideration.

However, this type of change takes on a new look once we get over the initial trauma of the divorce itself. Only then can we begin to realize its potential to make us wealthier. (In fact, fighting it out in court is as much a luxury as buying a yacht or a vacation home abroad.) This alone ought to crumble most of our resistance to the nice approach.

And, frankly, haven't we resisted worse changes in the past, changes which have gone on to become mainstays in our daily living? We don't even think about most of them anymore. Some have even cost us money or convenience, while being nice to our partner saves us money and inconvenience.

I'm talking about things like pumping our own gasoline and talking to robots with their endless menus of what number to press when we have a question about our electric bill. Or how about the worldwide acceptance of voice mail? Some of us will recall how we hated to talk into answering machines when they first came out.

Divorce Buddy System™

> All truth passes through three stages.
> First, it is ridiculed.
> Second, it is violently opposed.
> Third, it is accepted as being self-evident.
> —*Arthur Schopenhauer (1788-1860)*

Change happens. It's really more of a constant than a choice. Our only real choice has to do with when we allow ourselves to succumb to it . . . for we nearly always do. Sooner or later, we stop doing what doesn't work and start looking for something better. This is when change happens, and society and the divorce legal system are at exactly that point right now.

At their beginnings, we thought television was going to put radio out of business and VCRs were going to put an end to movie theatres. Right.

Remember when smoking in public places was the norm and smokers weren't treated like lepers? (I hasten to add that I have no axe to grind on this issue.) Recall those days when we did not have a coffee shop on every corner and coffee didn't cost five dollars a cup? How about when $25,000 was a lot of money to pay for a luxury car?

ATM, PIN, RV, SUV, and DVD: remember when these were alphabet soup? Or when cookies and blackberries were just things to eat? Or when we went places without carrying a bottle of water?

> An invasion of armies can be resisted
> but not an idea whose time has come.
> —*Victor Hugo (1802-1885)*

How did we ever survive without TiVo, debit cards, and on-line everything? And what about those male and female personal items we see advertised on TV? How did that happen?

The mention of these changes (and all their numerous counterparts) – whether we find them to be good, bad, or indifferent – serves to illustrate, when all is said and done, how adaptable we really are. There was a time when new technology amazed us, but we have now been amazed so often we tend to take the new stuff in stride.

Hopefully we will able to do the same when it comes to adjusting our mindset on the subject of divorce.

As George F. Will, the celebrated *Washington Post* columnist, puts it, "The future has a way of arriving unannounced."

You read it here first.

If you're still resisting the buddy system approach, please ask yourself these questions:

- Which do you dislike more: the prospect of being nice to your spouse or the prospect of throwing money away?

- Which of these would be more distasteful to you: being pleasant to someone who does not deserve it or giving money to someone who does not deserve it?

- Who would you rather give a new car to: your lawyer's kid or your own kid? Similarly, whose child would you prefer to put through college?

So, if your goal is to save money, keep reading. You're in the right place.

On the other hand, if you are hell-bent on dispensing some sort of slash-and-burn, carpet-bomb justice on your spouse, think for a moment: how much is it worth to you? Is it worth the cost of a new car?

Silent Might
>I have often regretted my words, never my silence.
>—*Xenocrates (396-314 BC)*

When either party in a divorce says or does the typical divorce-type things (e.g., making remarks that are insulting, belittling, childish, mean, rude, offensive or abusive), they should expect the same treatment in return. This leads to a downward spiral that should be avoided at all (of your) costs.

Divorce has an uncanny way of making grown adults act and sound like sniveling adolescents. So begin by forgiving yourself when you behave this way. It is perfectly normal under the circumstances, and even the best-intentioned find themselves sucked into this type of behavior. But that does not mean it will help your case!

You must stay away from this type of "one-downmanship." Remember, a closed mouth gathers no feet.

And consider this: when you are silent, you are depriving your spouse of something they would otherwise want to fight about. Silence leaves nothing to quarrel with, and nothing for the next negative thing to be built upon.

In the heat of the moment, when you are on the verge of fighting fire with fire, don't. That's right! Bite your tongue instead, and you may avoid winding up in ashes.

Never Put Your Mouth Where Your Money Is

Because what you say can and will be used against you. Utter the wrong thing now and you are likely to wind up paying for it later.

If you are self-defeating and do not watch what you say, you are likely to get exactly what you don't want, as you watch what you *do* want walk out the door with your spouse.

Instead, heed this valuable advice: the best way to eliminate any problem is proactively. In other words, prevent it. And the best way to prevent divorce problems is to

Act nicely toward your spouse, no matter what.

And the thought of treating our spouse nicely becomes more palatable when we look at the alternative, which is . . . there is none.

By fighting, you never get enough.
By yielding, you get more than you expect.

Now read on to learn how to "yield," so that you can finesse your way to a less painful and less expensive divorce.

SECTION III

How You Will Get through Your Divorce in One Peace

Chapter 5
Shake Hands & Come Out Negotiating

Let's assume you're at least willing to give the buddy system the old college try and act nicely toward your spouse, no matter what. Does this mean I'm recommending you just glue on a smile and say "yes" a lot?

Absolutely not. Knowing that we *should* act nicely and knowing *how* to act nicely are two different things. Neither society nor our common sense nor street smarts teach us *how* to act nicely within the context of divorce.

This nuts-and-bolts section begins the process of explaining precisely what we must say and do to get the job done.

We'll first become familiar with some basic professional negotiation and persuasion insights. These are the things they never told us about – the things that none of us would otherwise know to do or be willing to do.

Then we'll wade into three fundamentals – perspectives, emotions, and language/listening – that must be understood in order for you to derive the full value of the many specific tips located throughout the book.

Finally, we'll prepare for the unexpected by examining a laundry list of obstacles and curveballs, right through the last-minute trip wires that can blow things up at the very moment you expect to finalize the settlement.

Let's Make a Deal

Negotiation is the process we use to persuade others to give us something we want in exchange for something they want.

Persuasion is the method we use to get it (as opposed to using a gun, going to court, etc.).

Pure negotiation (as distinguished from haggling – more on that in Chapter 11) is a learned skill. It has come into its own in recent years and is now one of our more widely studied subjects. Negotiation and its sibling (or perhaps offspring), mediation, are extremely valuable tools in the business and legal communities. Both are now primary components of the curricula in the world's finest law schools and MBA programs.

The approach taught in *Divorce Buddy System* is a persuasion "booster rocket" that professional negotiators swear by. It is what they use to get their own spouses to say yes.

> Destroy your enemy by making him your friend.
> —Abraham Lincoln (1809-1865)

The best way to disarm your spouse is by respecting their stand. Your partner needs to tell their story and believe you finally understand it. (Remember Chapter 2, when we noted the basic human need to be understood?) This changes everything. Showing concern and respect for what they are saying reduces their anger and lack of trust. It relaxes their defenses and puts you in position to make a deal, sometimes without your spouse ever figuring out how you did it.

Irritable Spouse Syndrome

Despite the benefits of the non-confrontational approaches, many people still argue that these methods are naïve and don't stand a chance against human nature.

They believe the divorce experience triggers primitive responses within us, which, at the very least, block us from being able to bargain objectively. They contend that our "dark side" will laugh at friendly settlement overtures as being signs of weakness and trample them accordingly. They think we'd have more success trying to jump start Air Force One.

Frankly, I think there is something to be said for this gloomy view when it comes to Mean Gene spouses – those who are unreasonable, crazy, generally insufferable, terminally stubborn or otherwise impossible to deal with. This grouping always wants Wild West justice at any cost.

These are the difficult people who are afflicted with Irritable Spouse Syndrome (a very serious condition for which there is no known cure). They are also known as pit bulls, negotiation terrorists, cowboys, and gunslingers. They vomit at the mere mention of an anti-war approach to divorce, and to treat them nicely is a kiss of death.

Aside from these characters, there is also another brand of difficult litigant (also weaned on vinegar) with whom settlement is next to impossible. These are the parties that are unable to cope in situations where the applicable law differs from what they believe the law ought to be. They expect their personal sense of justice to prevail over the same legal standard that the rest of us are held to (whether we like it or not). They act as though what they *want* — and not the law — should determine what they *get*.

So beware. The secret applies to "reasonable" spouses only.

Define a "Reasonable" Spouse

My definition of a reasonable person, in the context of divorce negotiations, is someone who is capable of seeing their spouse's point of view.

How do you know if your spouse qualifies as "reasonable?" At this stage in the game, you may be having difficulty getting a handle on this. (You may not even be feeling very reasonable yourself.)

However, the answer is easily determined. Simply look back at your partner's general nature or behavior during the course of the marriage. Once a basically mean or argumentative person, always a basically mean or argumentative person. Once basically easygoing or non-confrontational, always basically easygoing or non-confrontational. And so on.

This does not mean you must agree with each of your spouse's positions. A reasonable person simply must be able to understand how the other person could conceivably think the way they do. A simple willingness to work with your spouse's thinking – even hypothetically, for the sake of argument – indicates that you are, indeed, taking their concerns and feelings into account. (And, frankly, once they sense you have made this crossover, your divorce is 75 percent settled.)

Does It Really Take Two to Tangle?

There's a common belief that it takes two to tangle but, in divorce, this is simply not true. It takes only one.

Yes, it does take two spouses to make a good marriage, but it takes only one obstinate spouse to make a divorce bad.

Just about every divorce case will descend to the level of its most difficult player, whether this is you, your partner – or even one of your lawyers! One troublesome participant can throw a monkey wrench into the deal. If your spouse is trouble, you're in trouble.

As we've learned, in many divorce cases, one (or sometimes both) of the partners is simply wired in such a way that the parties have little, if any, chance of ever reaching settlement. If you or your spouse is a difficult person, then your settlement discussions are, more likely than not, doomed from the start.

Difficult people come equipped with a built-in unwillingness to meet the other party halfway, and thus necessitate additional legal work. And, as you have already correctly surmised, extra legal work takes extra time and money.

Difficult people act like maniacs and then blame the legal system for taking too long and costing too much.

So don't waste your time, energy or resources trying to talk turkey to a donkey. Just get a good trial lawyer and take the advice you are given.

Don't Cut Off Your Nose to Spite Your Face

No matter how reasonable you and your spouse may be, we all have a volatile side and we must recognize how quickly it can surface – so quickly we rarely get any lag time in which to tailor our actions. And nothing brings out the monster faster than the insanity of divorce.

So we must be prepared to contain the beast, to anticipate its appearance, and be mindful of its power. It can make us say and do vicious, stupid, and unproductive things and this is never more than one remark away.

We can blow in a millisecond, and there are billions of milliseconds during the course of an entire divorce. This is how vulnerable we are and how vigilant we must be.

Our challenge, then, is to focus on settlement – keeping it in sight no matter what happens – and to recognize our own personal warning signs (e.g., a sudden dry mouth, tightening of stomach, adrenaline jitters, etc.), and try to be on the lookout for when we start to percolate.

In other words, remember the three major components for achieving a less painful, less expensive divorce:

1. Avoid aggravating your spouse.

2. Listen to what your spouse says and convince them you heard every word they said.

3. Know what to say and when to say it. Then say it nicely.

Now, every divorce is unique; each case involves different personalities and circumstances. What works for some partners with regard to the last two of the three major components may not work for others.

However, the application of the first major component is universal. It is the same for every party in every divorce: *Do not aggravate your spouse*, even if they deserve to be aggravated. Be nice even if they are murdering you with aggravation.

Instead, shake hands and come out negotiating.

Chapter 6
The Courthouse Door

As a young lawyer, I was taught that the best settlement device known to man is the courthouse door. Cases seem to drift until trial gets near. Once trial is imminent, settlement becomes everyone's priority.

In view of the fact that more than 90 percent of all divorce cases settle before trial – many on the eve of trial – I am confident that the courthouse door is still doing its job.

An old adage about achieving success in life holds that people do not drift *into* success; rather, they tend to drift *away* from success. If they want success to happen, they have to resist the tendency to drift.

I compare this to what happens when a divorce case enters our legal system. Unless the focus is on settlement, there is a tendency for a case to drift downriver (along with all the others in the logjam), until a year or two later, when it finally bumps into the courthouse door and gets everyone's attention.

The nice approach does what the courthouse door does. It creates an environment that puts settlement discussions on the front burner.

If You Build It, They Will Calm

But how do we create this environment? How do we let our spouse know that we are willing to do our part? And how do we act nicely toward someone who doesn't deserve it? Let's start with some basic *Dos* and *Don'ts*:

> **DO** use a calm and comforting tone of voice. This is an excellent tool for displaying sincerity and compassion.
>
> **DO** be respectful. People worry about their self-respect. They want to tell their friends and family they negotiated a good deal. Be sure your spouse leaves the table with some satisfaction and some bragging rights.
>
> **DON'T** give your partner a piece of your mind if you hope to get peace of mind.
>
> **DON'T** engage in self-defeating behavior such as closing or transferring accounts, hiding funds/assets, cutting off cash flow, running up charge cards, playing games with visitation, etc. This is a quick way to start a war, and even if your spouse isn't thinking about war, you just might cause one.
>
> **DON'T** make any negative remarks about your partner's vices, traits, propensities, habits, work tendencies, appearance, grooming, general behavior, and so on. Avoid the following and similar comments at all costs:
>
> - You've never finished anything you started.
>
> - When is the last time you did something with the kids?
>
> - I don't have any friends because you drove them all off.

Remember, your number one priority is to avoid aggravating your spouse. People who are not angry or otherwise emotionally charged are more open to considering solutions. Clear-mindedness makes it possible for your partner to see the problem as you do.

We should be aware of two things in particular that cause us to aggravate our spouse. Both are reactions that we can control once we acknowledge that they are in our blood, just waiting to cause trouble.

1. We don't know who we married.

Some of us sit down at the bargaining table and discover a whole new side to the person we married. So new, in fact, that we can't be sure if the person across the table is really our spouse or if it's some greedy creature from outer space that has taken over our spouse's form and brain.

The truth is that no one ever really knows who they married until a divorce gets underway. During their dating, courtship and marriage, the partners always have something to gain by ultimately smoothing out arguments or disagreements. It's as if there is some unwritten law that prevents the crossing of spousal behavior limits and friction boundaries.

Once divorce hits, all prior restraints disappear, and all speed limits are lifted. We are free to do whatever we want. And, this is when we get our first glimpse of who we married.

Recognize that you and the person you thought you knew best – and you thought knew you best – are now negotiating as strangers. You are both victims of the dynamics of divorce. *You overcome this by anticipating that you will not be able to anticipate what this "stranger" will do.* Expect the worst behavior imaginable, and you will not be tempted to overreact to anything your spouse throws your way.

2. We know we are right and they say we're wrong.

Don't ever tell us we are wrong when we know we are right. This is a real thorn in our side. If we are right (even when it's on a smaller point), we need our spouse to recognize that we are "right" or it will drive us crazy until they do.

This is an amazingly powerful human need that must be identified and respected. It is not something our pride, ego or pigheadedness allows us to debate.

We're likely to blow up the whole forest rather than give them this one tree. We are in trouble if our spouse doesn't comprehend the magnitude of this natural, non-negotiable propensity of ours. (I might add that we ought to be careful ourselves, because our spouse also happens to be afflicted with this natural, non-negotiable propensity.)

We have to accept that being right isn't why we're sitting at the bargaining table. We're there to resolve our problem, and not to add to it. The smart money says:

**Let your spouse be right today.
You can always be right after the money is divided.**

What is more important to you: the sabotaging insistence of the "my way or the highway" attitude or settling your divorce? Decide this early, because you are not going to get both.

Make Up Your Own House Rules

Another important means for creating a suitable negotiation environment is to invent your own house rules. Suggest that the two of you govern your conversations by mutually agreeing to the following:

- Only one of you will be allowed to get angry at the same time.

- If things get heated – no matter who is to blame – you will take a 20-minute break.
    o Either party can call a time-out; it must be honored INSTANTLY (this means mid-sentence, if need be) with no last words thrown in.

- The party speaking has the floor, and neither of you will interrupt or react as long as that person is speaking. They have the floor until they say they give it up.
    o If there is a silence, and only then, the other may ask for permission to speak. The proper question is "May I have the floor?"
        - Neither should ask questions like "Are you through?" or "Is it my turn now?"

- Neither of you will immediately judge the other's position as wrong but will keep the door open on a challenged issue until all your discussions have taken place and both of you have had the opportunity to explain yourselves fully.

- Neither of you will make any assumptions about the other's intentions or motives regarding their words or actions.
  - Our natural tendency is to assume they meant the worst, and this only aggravates the original problem. Blame itself is counterproductive, and accusing someone of intending to cause harm (especially when their motive was otherwise) is guaranteed to push them over the edge.

- Do not make the mistake of believing everything you think.

- Agree that anything that either of you says will be prefaced with an imaginary *if*. This is to facilitate the exchange of settlement positions and comments without either party becoming automatically bound by their own words.
  - For example, imagine something like this is said: "I think the house is worth $400,000, so I'll let you buy my one-half for $200,000."
  - Under this house rule, the parties will deem that statement to mean, "I'll accept $200,000 for my half…only *if* the house appraisal comes back at $400,000 or lower. The invisible *if* allows both parties to open up and start talking numbers without fear of having the numbers thrown back in their faces later in the negotiations.

- Agree in advance that if either party walks out, they must return the next day at the same time and place. Walking out does not end negotiations; it just ends them for that day.

- Agree you won't close an unsuccessful negotiation meeting with war words or word of finality. Agree in advance that you will both return and try again whenever you have an unpleasant meeting.

What your spouse is saying is important to them. Never brush off or minimize anything they say. Remember that in order to be heard, you must first listen.

Isn't it remarkable that *listen* and *silent* are spelled with the same letters?

This does not mean you have to agree with your partner. But it's critical that you acknowledge his or her point of view – no matter how right you may be. Keep in mind that the louder your bark, the larger your legal bill.

So, right now, zero in on the importance of managing your emotions. You can always explain true justice to your spouse later, when it's less costly to do so. In the meantime, play by the house rules and never forget to request a break if you sense your emotions starting to percolate.

In a successful divorce settlement, each partner gives up something they want in order to make the settlement attractive to the other. Until we are ready to do this, a settlement is next to impossible, and we typically do not reach this point until the daily torment of divorce finally wears us down.

Please note that I said "finally wears us down." We do not shed our expectations and emotional baggage overnight. It can take time – more time than an early settlement typically permits.

Simply being aware of this helps you to endure it. Here are some questions to ask yourself as you move through the process:

- What is really causing me to refuse to budge?

- Am I getting my wants confused with my needs?

- Exactly what am I resisting here? And why am I resisting it?

- Do I want to be arguing about this same thing a year from now? (This is also a great question to ask your spouse!)

Take the Pulse

Always check out your partner's mood. The last thing you want to do is try to make a point or ask for something if your spouse is in a particularly resistant state of mind.

But remember: your soon-to-be ex will find it hard to discredit or attack someone who is agreeing with them. Typically, they will not stop resisting until you lead the way and start agreeing first.

And so we find ourselves with another set of *Do*s and *Don't*s:

DO adopt early settlement as a goal and ask your partner to do the same.

DO tread softly at the beginning of negotiations. A helpful atmosphere created right from the start is vital to your overall chances of settlement.

DO warm up your spouse and get on their good side (as best you can) before talking about money.

DO try to find some common ground that the two of you can agree upon. In fact, generally try to do this whenever you can. Write these items on a piece of paper and keep them face up on the table for both of you to see.

DON'T let friends or family put pressure on you to feel a certain way or tell you what your settlement position ought to be. Their intentions are good, but their knowledge of the law probably isn't.

DON'T propose anything to your partner until you are sure the coast is clear and they are in a decent mood.

There's more to the buddy system "nice approach," of course – we're about to begin exploring three major factors (perspective, emotions, and language/listening) that will help you see the much larger picture.

If you can pull off just one of the helpful hints in the next chapter, you'll be way ahead of most people going through a divorce.

And a lot farther from the courthouse door.

Chapter 7
The Blinding Power of Perspectives

The most useful (and least recognized) tool in dispute resolution is being able to understand why your partner sees things differently.

Remember the three major components to acting nicely toward your spouse (Chapter 4)? The blinding power of perspectives has to do with the second part:

Listen to what your spouse says and convince them you heard every word they said.

In fact, this is a major key to unlocking the rest of the doors. So it is vital – imperative – that we gain some understanding of the powerful forces that perspectives bring to the negotiation process.

By definition, *perspective* is how we see or understand something. It's our point of view. What we see is what we believe.

What most of us don't recognize about perspectives is that they are very deeply seated and thus cannot easily be changed. In fact, we dig in deeper when someone challenges our viewpoint.

Perspectives are involuntary, subjective, and extremely personal. They are formed over the years by our life experiences, and they affect our thinking at every level.

Who Gets a Raw Deal – Men or Women?

Here are two examples to illustrate how basic perspectives can be. First, I invite you to ask any male friend or family member:

Do you believe women get a raw deal in divorce?

Or, switch it around, and ask any female if she thinks men get a raw deal in divorce?

The people I have asked not only answer no; they also get a look on their faces suggesting it would be moronic for anyone to answer otherwise. Their automatic no is the result of years of subconscious data entry.

Now a second, less generalized example: Bill Clinton's behavior in the White House. The public – all with the same information to go on – judged the significance of his actions differently.

Some claimed Mr. Clinton's behavior had a lot to do with nothing, and some thought it had a lot to do with everything.

Why didn't the same input lead us all to the same opinion? Because we have differing perspectives. Each member of our society judged Mr. Clinton's behavior through their own highly personal perspective lens. We saw only what our lens allowed us to see. If we liked him, we saw one thing; if we didn't like him, we saw another thing.

This example helps explains what a perspective is. Now, to get a sense of perspective's power, please consider this further question: if we broke those who felt strongly about the Clinton controversy into two camps, with 10 million people in one camp believing what he did was a big deal, and 10 million people in the second camp believing it was not a big deal, how many people in either camp do you think could be convinced to change their mind at the urging of someone from the other camp?

Few? Probably none. This is true power, and this is why it is so hard to change our spouse's mind.

Why Should I Care What My Spouse Thinks?

Once we have a perspective, anything we observe is seen with this perspective in mind. When we notice things that confirm the righteousness of our view, we accept them as evidence that our perspective is correct. When something does not confirm our view, we minimize or ignore it.

The more convinced we are of our view, the more we tend to filter out information that would lead us to question our underlying assumptions. Thus, the more entrenched our perspective, the more obvious it is to us that we are right and our partner is wrong. The hardest mind to pry open is usually our own. Am I saying your spouse is actually in the right? Not at all. Your spouse merely sees things in a way that benefits them, while we see things in a way that benefits us. This is human nature.

We do not see things as they are; we see things as *we* are.

But why should you care about our partner's perspective? Isn't that the magic of divorce, the freedom not to care what they think?

Not yet it isn't. Not as long as you need your spouse's signature. Freedom and peace of mind may be just on the other side of the minefield, but we have to get there in one piece.

Are There Really Two Sides to Every Story?

As a responsible author, I am supposed to give a resounding yes to that question. Speaking as a human, however, I must admit that I have my doubts.

Therefore, my official answer is this: if we are talking about your problem, there are indeed two sides. If it is my problem, there is really only one side. I have found it profitable, however, to pretend that there could be two.

If your spouse has a different perspective, understand that different does not mean *wrong*. It only means *different*.

Explain this reality to your spouse and ask for a mutual agreement allowing both of your perspectives to sit at the bargaining table with the two of you. Arguing is futile, so set a couple of extra chairs.

In other words, hear these words and embrace this concept:

You will never be able to change your spouse's perspective, and your spouse will never be able to change yours!

It cannot be done. Our divorce courts are jammed with angry litigants who cannot understand how their spouse can remain so stubborn and impossible to deal with. But they are wasting their time trying to bulldoze through their partner's perspective. They should be using their energy to figure out a way around it.

This is because, when you and your spouse are stuck, one of you must make the first move to get unstuck. Are you willing to bet $25,000 to $50,000 in attorney fees that your spouse will be that person?

The Boulder

A perspective can be compared to a massive boulder blocking the entire width of a two-lane highway.

Imagine that you and your spouse are traveling in opposite directions (coming toward one another) on this highway, and that a boulder has rolled down to block all passage. The two of you reach the boulder at the same time and come to a full stop with your respective front bumpers right up against opposite sides of the boulder.

The boulder must be moved before either of you will be able to proceed toward your destination. So you both try to nudge the boulder out of the way by slowly moving your autos forward, but your mutual counter resistance prevents all forward movement. You both want to go on your way but the boulder prevents you. So what do you do?

You must both accept that you will not be able to budge the boulder. If you want to get where you are going, you will have to go around it.

In like fashion, you will never be able to budge your spouse's perspective because what they perceive, they believe. So, if you want to reach a settlement, you will have to do what you did with the boulder and find a way around it. Getting around the boulder requires the cooperation of both parties and this is where acting nicely pays off.

If you want to know how impossible it is to actually change someone's perspective, think about how impossible it would be for your spouse to change the way you see things. Then reverse it. What's good for the goose is also good for the other goose.

Getting Around the Boulder

Listening to your spouse's perspective is painful. After all, you know they are seeing things "incorrectly," and you aren't.

However, the real source of the pain lies in the frustration that comes from trying to get your partner to see things your way. Since this is never going to happen, accept it as another one of life's bitter truths and watch your pain and frustration begin to lessen. Accepting this reality lightens your load and gives you a nice sense of freedom. It is much easier to accept something if we realize it was never within our control to begin with.

So, how do we get around the boulder?

> **DO** force yourself to be curious about your spouse's perspective. Try to make a space in your mind to store their viewpoint along with your own.
>
> **DO** display keen interest in your partner's concerns. When they make a proposal you don't agree with, do not shoot it down in its infancy.
>
> **DO** ask for an explanation of the feelings that governed their thinking while they were developing their proposal. Once you learn their feelings, attempt to dig deeper for further elaboration.
>
> **DO** ask, "What are your concerns?" This goes much further than saying, "Here's what I think is fair."
>
> **DO** remember that it does not cost you to "allow" your spouse to have a differing viewpoint. Show that you are receptive to hearing it and that you will try to understand it.
>
> **DO** remember that your spouse has had different life experiences, and it is perfectly normal for them to see things differently.

Heart and Soul

Skillfully dealing with differences in our perspectives is the real heart and soul of conflict management. We must accept that it is normal for our spouse to see the world in a way that favors their position, and it is our job to deal with what they see.

Notice I said *deal*, not *accept*. It is *not* necessary for us to accept our partner's perspective. However, it *is* necessary for us to understand it as it is, and *not* as what we think it is or what we wish it to be. It is impossible to gain such an understanding without first listening to what they are trying to tell us.

While perspectives play a major role in divorce settlement discussions and are deadly all on their own, they are only a part of the problem. They share center stage with two other, equally important, fundamentals – emotions and language/listening – which are coming up next.

Chapter 8
Emotions: Disturbing the Peace

Emotions are not something we think; they are something we feel. In divorce, negative emotions – fear, jealousy, anger, frustration, and resentment – commonly arise when we believe we are being wronged or when we believe something we value is being threatened. Emotions trump logic and, more often than not, cause us to say and do things we later regret.

Having strong emotions during the divorce process is unavoidable, but how we handle them is up to us. We can keep them on a short leash.

And we must recognize that emotions have the same effect on our spouse as they do on us. It makes sense, therefore, to try to reduce the intensity of our partner's negative emotions by controlling how we show our own.

In this chapter, we'll get to know more about two of divorce's most devastating negative emotions – anger and anxiety.

Jack of All Tirades
>Whatever is begun in anger ends in shame.
>—*Benjamin Franklin (1706-1790)*

"I was so angry, I couldn't think straight." True words indeed.

Anger is our most powerful emotion, and the anger we experience in divorce is pure poison. It is an overpowering, specialized, and intense form of anger that we have not felt before. It is a form of temporary insanity that catches us off guard and turns us into a monster. And, while pleading insanity may work in a criminal case, it doesn't help us in divorce.

Anger is the universal language of divorce. Or, more accurately, anger is the universal language of those who are headed for a long and expensive divorce.

We seem to feel more entitled to display anger at home than we do at school, work or elsewhere. We recognize the value of trying to control our temper when we're out of the house (exploding in front of co-workers, neighbors, customers, etc.). Not so, however, when it comes to blowing our top in front of the soon-to-be-ex. Here, we feel no compunction about acting like we're in Dodge City.

Here are some of the effects of showing our anger:

- It makes us look crazy.
- It closes our spouse's ears and prevents us from making our point.
- It distorts our perception, twists our thinking, and impairs our ability to solve problems.
- It gives our partner justification to see themselves as a victim.

This last point is especially significant. Victims believe they deserve revenge, and we don't want to negotiate our financial futures with someone who feels it is their turn to inflict punishment.

Incidentally, being unable to get our spouse to see things as we do is often enough to trigger our own feelings of victimization; the same holds true when we realize we don't control things. This happens whenever another person (our spouse, the judge, etc.) has the power to determine what we're entitled to.

Blamer v. Blamer

One of the biggest sources of anger is blame.

In fact, blame and anger work hand in hand. If we are angry, we blame; and placing blame intensifies our anger. The person we blame resents being blamed, so they follow suit and get angry back. They blame us (or our reaction) for their anger, thus adding to the downward spiral.

The angrier we both become, the further we get from reaching a settlement. Someone has to break this reactive pattern. Unfortunately, this is usually the last thing that angry people are willing to do.

The thing about anger and blame is that neither can get us what we want.

You must remember this when your spouse is breathing fire and your eyebrows are getting singed. It is imperative that you not add to the flames. Anger feeds off itself, and one of you must take the initiative to stop it from spreading. Make yourself temper proof.

But how?

Cat Should Get Your Tongue

We must sharpen our view of what is at stake and keep our eye on the prize – less pain, less expense – at all times. Control the encounter or it will control you. Never give your spouse access to your hot buttons, and don't trust your impulses. Angry people make bad decisions. Don't get mad; get shrewd.

Never, ever get hooked by your spouse's anger.

Easier said than done? Not really. There is one simple thing we can all do to contain our anger: anticipate theirs. Know your partner *is* going to lose it; expect them to attack suddenly and hard. Anticipate fury, and you will be able to handle fury – without unleashing your own.

Try to create lag time before responding to one of your spouse's shots. You do this by waiting three seconds before speaking in answer to anything your spouse says. This is a good habit to get into generally and is really helpful in providing "cool down" time.

Reason has little power against anger.

When things are really threatening to go over the top, you may need a longer time-out. It can, in fact, take up to twenty minutes for clear thinking to return, so excuse yourself from the room for a quick break and splash water on your face. If this isn't practical, distance yourself from the situation for at least a little while by pretending you left something in the car.

When it's time to talk again, try saying something like, "Look, I know this may not be going too well. Frankly, I'm kind of frustrated. If we're going to resolve this, I know I have to put my feelings aside and try to work on some alternatives. Are you with me on this?"

Or, another good way to cool things down (and feel proud of yourself) when you feel your blood starting to boil is to say something like, "If it's okay with you, I'd like to go over your objectives again. It's easy for me to get off track, and I want to be sure I'm not losing sight of what is important to you."

When your spouse explodes, wait patiently for them to stop talking, and then simply say the six miracle words.

The Six Miracle Words
I can hear you are upset.

This is a miracle sentence indeed, doing several things that defending ourselves will never accomplish.

These six little words

- establish that we were listening
- acknowledge our spouse's right to have such an opinion
- do not say their opinion is wrong, and
- do not say that we agree or disagree with them.

These six miracle words prevent our partner's anger from escalating – and stops ours from beginning.

When our spouse starts in with their litany of injustices, we feel a need to set the record straight and defend ourselves. But we now know that we can't change our spouse's mind by disagreeing with them. Challenging their accusations cannot help us; it will only add to our frustration and make us angrier. Instead, we simply say to our spouse, "I can hear you are upset."

This is one hundred times better than defending ourselves in the normal way. Remember, explosions do not put things together. When the other side explodes and lets anger get the best of them, let it go. Expect your spouse to lose it at least twice during the divorce. And don't take it personally when they do. *Ask yourself how returning their fire will further your cause.* The meaning of your message is lost when it cannot be heard over the racket.

Defending ourselves or arguing with our spouse during negotiations makes about as much sense as trying to turn off a lamp by throwing bricks at it.

We can profit from our spouse's explosions only if we do not react in kind. When they explode, stay cool for as long as you can. Realize that the moments after a blow-off provide you with a wonderful opportunity to enter a zone where resolution becomes possible.

Having let off steam, your partner will become calmer and more willing to listen to your side of the story than ever before – particularly when you remember to use the six magic words: "I can hear you are upset."

Minimum Rage

Yes, it is impossible to keep anger out of divorce, but it is not impossible to learn how to control it.

> **DO** recognize the need to manufacture lag time before responding when your spouse presses your buttons. Creating lag time seems difficult, but waiting three seconds isn't. Focus on the three seconds, and the rest takes care of itself.
>
> **DO** disconnect from your anger if you hope to get your spouse to see things your way. Anger doesn't sell anyone on anything.
>
> **DO** keep your cool. When your spouse gets mad, don't get mad back. Never respond by saying things like, "Don't you dare talk to me in that tone."

DO tell yourself how much their outburst is going to help the chances of settlement. Most settlements don't occur until at least one blow-off per spouse has happened.

We have the right to be difficult, but not if we want our divorce to be quick and inexpensive. We can't have it both ways.

DO look at the big picture when your blood starts to boil. Look at the negotiations as a whole – as if they were a forest. If your spouse is unreasonable on one or two terms, don't isolate them in your mind. See them as just one or two trees in an otherwise healthy forest.

DON'T fight anger with anger. Angry spouses lose negotiations. You can't lessen their anger until you can control your own. Remember "sticks and stones" from when you were a child?

DON'T use words that are wolves in sheep's clothing or ask questions that are statements in disguise (e.g., "Is it okay if I splurge and buy a quarter pound of bologna on my birthday?"). This is the worst time for smart-aleck remarks or levity of any type.

DON'T insert humorous remarks when your spouse is being serious. This only gives them more cause to be difficult.

DON'T make statements that have the effect of proclaiming your entitlement and/or your spouse's lack of entitlement, such as, "The pension is all mine. I worked for it." Those statements are surefire troublemakers.

DON'T challenge or insult your spouse or anything that they say. Sentences such as "How can you just sit there and lie?" or "Maybe if you came home sober once in a while" or "Maybe if I ever came home and found dinner on the table" will only bring you closer to an in-court battle.

You can definitely gain monetarily if you can disengage from your emotions.

Your anger is your spouse's best weapon.

Post-Romantic Stress
> Anxiety: painful uneasiness over an impending ill;
> a state of uneasiness and apprehension
> about future uncertainties
> —*American Heritage Dictionary*

Divorce is about loss. It threatens what we value the most – our family, our cash flow, our standard of living, our future, our stability, even the way we feel about ourselves. To say that anxiety is inevitable in divorce is putting it mildly. Divorce is pure stress, pure agony.

How could we not feel strong emotion – anxiety, created by fear and doubt – when we don't know the answers to crucial questions such as these?

> *Will we have to sell the house?*
> *Will the kids have to switch schools?*
> *Will I have to move, and where will I go?*
> *What will I be able to afford?*
> *What will I do for a living?*
> *Who will hire me?*
> *What if I lose my job?*
> *How will I pay my bills?*
> *How will I pay support and still be able to live?*
> *Will I be able to afford health insurance?*
> *What if my income drops next year?*

Full Court Stress
Anxiety prevents us from communicating effectively because it freezes our mind in the closed position and makes it hard for us to get

our point across. Anxiety also prevents us from comprehending what we need to comprehend when others speak.

What can we do to mitigate our very understandable anxiety?

The best way is to avoid arguing with our spouse. Non-confrontational communication with our soon-to-be-ex can go a long way toward reducing their anxiety before it can gain any momentum. And, if we reduce theirs, we reduce ours. We win the war if we can prevent it from starting.

By taking the lead and refusing to respond to arguing with more arguing, we may inspire our spouse to follow suit. Does that guarantee they will reciprocate? No, but firing away at them with both barrels does guarantee they'll fire right back.

Arguing is always futile. It's a waste of breath, and it just makes our partner dig in deeper.

> Nine times out of ten, an argument ends with
> each of the contestants more firmly convinced
> than ever that he or she is absolutely right.
> —Dale Carnegie (1888-1955)

Anxiety in divorce arises out of perfectly reasonable concerns that people have about their financial security or entitlement. The best chance we have at reducing our spouse's anxiety is to be as reasonable as we can when addressing their worries. No one ever told us how vital this is.

Imagine how many of us have unwittingly caused our own divorce disasters by not knowing to show respect for our partner's beliefs and concerns. Instead, we did what our culture told us to do: We immediately challenged their viewpoint and tried to talk them into accepting ours.

Once again, the key to the buddy system is to act nicely and with respect and understanding.

The Weary Traveler

Imagine a weary and frustrated traveler whose flight has just landed four hours late. When he arrives at his hotel, he is informed by the desk clerk that his room has been given away, even though the guest had called before boarding his flight to say he'd be late, and the clerk on duty had assured him the room would be held for his arrival. Now, at three o'clock in the morning, he is room-less, it is snowing, and there are no cabs.

The desk clerk politely explains that he was obliged to follow the hotel's policy of not holding rooms after midnight. The guest is also told that the clerk, who promised to hold the room, was now off duty; and, to make matters worse, the clerk was not authorized to make such a promise in the first place.

At this point, the guest needs someone to understand what he is going through and how undeserving he is of this raw deal. He didn't cause the flight to be late, and he even called to say he would be late. He did everything he was supposed to do.

The desk clerk, by responding defensively and proclaiming his innocence, has done little to ease the situation.

How should he have handled it?

In the same way you should handle your spouse's frustration and anger.

Never, ever offer excuses, proclaim your innocence or defend yourself. Your spouse is hurting, and the pain won't go away just because you didn't intend to cause it or because the incident was not your fault or because you were just doing your job.

What the upset traveler and your upset partner need is someone to take their side. They need us to understand their pain, and that we fully justify their feeling it. They need compassion.

Peace by Peace

Sympathy, empathy, and compassion all denote the tendency or capacity to share in the feelings of others, especially their distress, sorrow or unfulfilled desires.

Sympathy is the broadest of these terms, signifying a general kinship with another's feelings. Empathy generally refers to the ability to imagine oneself in another's shoes. Compassion implies a deep concern for the troubles of others, coupled with a desire to alleviate their distress.

All three show respect for your spouse's position, without invalidating yours and without actually validating theirs. In fact, you do not actually have to *feel* the compassion. You merely have to sound like you do.

The Peace Academy

We'll talk much more in the next chapter about how to listen and how to use language to accomplish this. But, in the meantime, here are some helpful *Do's* and *Don't*s:

> **DO** show understanding for your partner's position. Compassion and understanding stimulate compassion and understanding. What you give may come back buttered.
>
> **DO** step back from your spouse's emotional outbursts, verbal barrages, innuendos, hateful looks, etc.
>
> **DO** look at things from a different angle. Pretend you are in the balcony watching two actors playing you and your partner on the stage below. The same words that would normally get us heated up can sound downright laughable when the actors say them.
>
> **DO** treat your spouse with dignity. Your spouse may just decide to return the favor.
>
> **DO** show your partner that you are willing to compromise. They may just decide to reciprocate.
>
> **DO** refrain from defending yourself. Don't even think about it.
>
> **DON'T** ever say that you pity your spouse, because that is condescending. Pity suggests sorrow for others who are generally less fortunate – and this is not the time you want your spouse to feel less fortunate.
>
> **DON'T** ramble on about how you didn't mean to hurt your spouse. This does not cheer them up one bit.
>
> **DON'T** tell your spouse what they should do. Don't say things like, "Here's what I think you should do," or

Divorce Buddy System™

"Oprah always says you should . . . ." Offering a solution makes you sound like you have all the answers, and it puts your partner on the defensive.

Instead, say assuring things like, "Let's try to figure this out," or "I think we are both reasonable, so let's put our heads together and try to find a middle ground" or "I'm sure we can do what it takes to solve this."

DON'T try to fix or repair your spouse's feelings. Just acknowledge them as valid. This will go a long way in the negotiation process.

Stay away from things like, "You're feeling destitute? You shouldn't feel destitute" or "Just look at the bright side" or "How can you be mad? I'm the one being taken to the cleaners here."

It would serve you better simply to say, "This must be hard for you."

DON'T ever respond to something your spouse says with a remark like "Whatever" or "Do what you want." Nobody wants to hear a snotty or flippant retort when they are in pain. Talk about incendiary! This is like using a flamethrower in a dry forest.

Compassion means that you show respect for the plight of your partner (a plight much like your own). It can work like an exhaust fan and draw the pain out of the room. And we all know that pain lies at the heart of every divorce dispute. Tranquilize that pain, and you will tranquilize the dispute.

Compassion cannot always make things better, but a failure to show (or at least feign) compassion *always* makes things worse. If nothing else, it is good business to make a sincere effort to sympathize with our spouse's plight. If we fail to transmit compassion, the chance of reaching a less expensive – and less painful – settlement will decrease drastically.

And the most effective way to transmit compassion is by putting to work the second and third major components of the buddy system's nice approach. This is the subject of the next chapter, where we learn to

- Listen to what our spouse says, convince them we heard every word they said, and know what to say and when to say it.

- Then say it nicely.

Chapter 9
Language & Listening:
Now Ear This

Nobody ever listened themselves out of a job.
—President Calvin Coolidge (1872-1933)

You can, however, listen yourself right into a less painful, less expensive divorce. This chapter is aimed at showing you how to talk (and listen) your way out of a divorce war.

As the Word Turns

Words, you see, are your most effective weapons in reaching a settlement – the right words, spoken at the right time, in the right way, and the words you listen to and respond to appropriately.

The pain that divorcing spouses experience is impossible to suppress for very long. We wear it on our sleeves and express it through our language. This hinders our ability to think and interact constructively. Communicating nicely with your spouse will ease their pain, and will likely ease yours, too.

The language that will affect the outcome of your divorce consists of three critical elements: wording, tone of voice, and body language.

Non-Friction Diction

We have to watch the language we use (or do not use). Yes, those dirty little deal-killing words pop up when we least expect them, and most of us are unaware of the devastation they bring.

Surprisingly, one of the worst offenders is *you are*, more commonly spoken as *you're*. It makes *you* – the person being addressed (now at the end of a figuratively pointed finger) – see the pirate's flag of attack. No other single word or phrase will result in faster or harder retaliation than the accusing *you're*. Your spouse will quickly bring out the big guns in retaliation the moment he or she hears any of the following:

> *You're not cooperating.*
> *You're always argumentative.*
> *You're never happy.*
> *You're the problem.*
> *You're, you're, you're . . .*

Use this nasty little contraction, and *you're* destined to be your own worst enemy. *You're* sure to be in a lot of trouble before you even begin, and *you're* going to be lucky if you walk away with the stick the flag was on!

Make *I* statements, not *you* statements. For example, do not say, "You are nuts if you think I am going to pay $4,000 a month." Instead, say, "I am seriously jolted by the $4,000 figure. I think I might be a little stunned." You will still be voicing your disapproval, but you will not be antagonizing your spouse.

The essence of this subtle difference is that *I* statements say, "I'm the one with the problem," but *you* statements point the finger and imply that the other person is the one with the problem, which puts them on the defensive.

Remember the old saying, "An ounce of prevention is worth a pound of cure?" There is a reason why certain sayings last for generations. They have proven themselves true, time and time again. Sometimes it only takes a few well-chosen words to change the tone and direction of divorce negotiations – and prevent pounds of pain.

He Said, She Said

Each partner in a divorce has their own story. How can we discuss these differences without reaching for the nitroglycerin?

One sure way is to make our point in the third person. If an unaffected third person were to report on both positions, he or she would talk about the differences between the two versions without making a judgment about either. We should try to do the same.

For example, let's say your spouse criticizes your untidiness. A constructive response would go something like this:

> I see we have *different* thoughts about my household habits. Your thought seems to be that I don't pick up after myself, and my thought is different; I think that I do. I wonder if we can talk about reaching a happy medium – you know; something that will work for both of us.

Differences are of a neutral value. You're not judging your spouse's opinion and you're not beating them over the head with yours. You're simply noting the *difference* of opinion. (By the way, be sure to say the word *different* at least twice.)

When we are insulted – *You never picked up a dirty sock in your life!* – our instinct is to insult back. We should expect flak from our partner because flak is one of the more predictable things in divorce. "Shame on us" if we get caught off guard by something we should know is coming. (More on this in Chapter 10, Incoming, Incoming)

The Speakers of the House – Getting Your Spouse to Open Up

"Opening up the lines of communication" is a phrase with which we're all familiar, but how do we actually accomplish this?

Your spouse wants to tell you what they think, but they may not have the communication skills to do it effectively. They may also be especially wary of opening up to you, which makes your job twice as challenging.

The answer is to ask questions in response to your spouse's strong statements. For example, your spouse says "I'm telling you up front, I want $50,000, and I'm not going below that." A suggested response would be "I respect your trying to negotiate in good faith, and I'm really not differing with you. But, it's important that I know where you're coming from, so please help me to understand how you reached this number. What factors did you consider?

Questions effectively encourage communication because they avoid negativity and demonstrate that you are listening to learn their side (and not to judge or challenge it).

You may find the following questions very effective in helping your partner open up to you:

- I would like to talk about this some more. How about you?
- Do I understand you correctly? You're saying . . .
- I hear what you're saying, but I must ask what I can do to help prove to you that my heart is in the right place?
- Can you give me some examples that will help me understand your feelings better?
- Could you elaborate?
- What do you say we try to come up with something creative – something that we might both be able to live with?
- Are you willing to help me try to come up with just one more way of settling this? Something we haven't considered before?
- What is the main thing that is stopping you from agreeing?
- What concerns you the most?
- What do you see as a possible stumbling block to our wrapping this up?
- Is there a number that would make you feel comfortable?
- Within reason, what would I have to do to get you to say yes?
- Can we make a list of the things that we do agree on?
- Is there any information you need from me that would make your decision easier?

And don't forget the "house rule" (see Chapter 6) that puts an imaginary *if* in front of anything that either of you says.

Always try to ask all your questions in the proper tone of voice. Concern and sincerity can be reflected through inflection and pitch – as can lack of concern and insincerity. Tone of voice can move you in the right direction or back you into a corner.

Tones of voice are contagious. Adopt the same pace of speech that your spouse uses. Please keep in mind that the way you ask for something can be just as important as what you are asking for in the first place.

We've already been reminded how using the right words can help soften our tone. We must always keep in mind, though, that even the best non-reactive questions can hurt us if we use the wrong tone when asking them.

The questions should not sound like you are challenging or confronting what your spouse says. Rather, use a tone of voice that demonstrates you genuinely wish to know more about what they are saying. Show them with your pitch and inflection that you want a clear understanding of their position and that you want to be sure your understanding is correct. Always speak calmly and evenly.

And don't forget volume. Resist the tendency to speak loudly because it is truly one of the worst things you can do. No one is ever listens to someone who is trying to make their point in a loud voice. Ironically, those who get loud, think the other party won't listen to them unless they are loud.

He Hears Me, She Hears Me Not

> Talk to people about themselves
> and they will listen for hours.
> —*Benjamin Disraeli (1804-1881)*

The way to persuade our spouse to be reasonable is by listening to why they think *their* position is reasonable. Explaining the reasonableness of our position won't get us very far. It's like trying to plow water.

As we've learned, one reason that settlement attempts fail is that, with our biased view of things, we see only our own "truth." This prevents us from comprehending how the other side might see things differently. We focus so intently on the truth we are trying to explain, that we block ourselves from hearing the truth they are trying to explain. And here's the real truth:

**We will persuade our spouse to be reasonable
by listening to what they need to say,
not by saying what we think needs to be said.**

Our soon-to-be-ex does not care about what we feel or think. They only care about what they feel and think. By the time our settlement conversations begin, they have already turned off their hearing aids. This is why we do not win arguments by talking.

**No one ever changes their mind
until they have been listened to.**

Incidentally, if you are wondering whether this listening stuff is actually effective, you are in good company. Most everyone challenges its simplicity at first. But believe it. This is powerful medicine. This is your velvet sledgehammer.

I'm All Ears
Why do we become hard of hearing during divorce settlement conversations? Here are the main reasons:

- We know what our spouse is going to say, and we know it supports their view and not ours.

- We know what they are going to say, and we know they are wrong.

- We do much of our so-called listening merely to give us ammo for a "Yes, but . . ." response or to find something to attack. We selectively listen for those things that will prove our point.

- We don't give two hoots about what they think or why they think it and can't stand listening to a view that is contrary to our own.

Knock Three Times

Remember in Chapter 8 we talked about defusing anger by waiting three seconds before responding? Well, this short delay is also used to indicate that we were listening to our partner all the while. It shows respect because it signals that we wanted extra time to let their words to sink in.

Quick responses are signs of poor listening, so counting to three before replying is a good habit to get into.

Be the one who is learning, not the one who is teaching.

Without specific instruction and guidance, we normally waste all our energy trying to talk some sense into someone who isn't listening. True, you have the right to speak your piece, but you don't have the right to make anyone listen. This is something that must be earned.

Don't talk about yourself or about what you want until you ask to hear your spouse's viewpoint – and you have listened to it fully and with compassion. This is the only way to soften up your partner. You can't convince anyone you have listened carefully to what they have to say, if all you do during the settlement meeting is talk about *your* view, what *you* want, and what *you* need.

When we show we are willing to open our mind to something new, it makes it easier for our partner to follow suit.

The more you say, the less your spouse will hear.

Think everyone listens to what he or she hears? Unfortunately, they don't. Listening and hearing are not the same. Hearing without actually listening runs rampant in divorce settlement discussions.

Why? Because we listen all wrong. We listen for something to criticize, and we listen for our spouse to say something that will prove our point. This will not keep us out of divorce court. Hearing is easy but listening is work.

Listening is much more than waiting for a turn to speak.

Even under non-divorce circumstances, we have a natural tendency to discount what we don't want to hear. If we try this in divorce, we are substituting the buddy approach with the kamikaze approach. Listening is the largest part of what it takes to settle a divorce case. We must first listen in order to be heard. It all starts there.

Listening is the cheapest concession we can make.

Friendly Persuasion

Persuasion is a process that normally takes more than one sit-down. A process is not the same as a light switch. In this case, the process involves taking measures to learn how to get the message through to your spouse's wiring. Then you flip the switch.

Anticipate that the two of you will not see eye to eye at the beginning, and force yourself to be patient. We cannot eat an elephant in one sitting.

Explain to your spouse at the start of negotiation discussions that you will make every attempt to be respectful even if you disagree with something they say. Explain that we all have a tendency to react to something we don't agree with and acknowledge that these reactions are harmful to the resolution process.

Then, as you proceed, put into action these *Do's* and *Don't*s of effective use of language and listening:

> **DO** give your spouse ample opportunity to explain how they see things. At the very start, they need to speak for at least 45 seconds straight in order to sense that you care about hearing their side.
>
> **DO** acknowledge their point of view and agree with them whenever you can. However, preface your statements of agreement in light of your experiences. For example, "I can see why you are asking such a stiff price. That makes sense based on what you have been told, but my experience brings me to a different conclusion . . ."
>
> **DO** keep in mind that if you must mention your spouse's objectionable behavior, do so only in the context of how the behavior affects you. For example, if your spouse accuses you of being greedy, respond by saying, "I feel

hurt and frustrated when I hear you say something like this." It gets your point across without your having to challenge their words.

DO anything you can to stop or reverse things when the discussion takes a downturn. Say, "This means a lot to me, but I'm afraid I may have derailed myself. I would sure like to start over again; is that okay? I promise not to go in the same direction I just did."

DON'T tell your spouse what is fair. "Fair" is something that exists in your mind only and is of little importance to your spouse. What are the odds of someone ever saying "Of course, I'll accept your proposal; I would be nuts to question something you have decreed to be fair"?

DON'T stonewall your partner. This is when you flat-out reject their position as being ridiculous. We can stonewall both by ignoring them or by saying things like, "Do what you want. See if I give two hoots."

DON'T anticipate what your spouse will say next. In other words, don't mentally jump ahead to what you think their next point will be.

DON'T generalize your spouse's position to be only what you expect it to be. Listen hard to fully comprehend everything that is said.

DON'T offer interpretations of your spouse's behavior. Forget statements like, "You weren't calling to talk to the kids. You were just checking to see if I went out with my friends. I deserve a life, too!"

DON'T impose your values upon your spouse with statements like, "A decent person wouldn't do what you did" or "Maybe the children should know that their father/mother has no morals."

DON'T register disapproval of anything your spouse says with facial expressions or body language.

DON'T attack your spouse's offer, and don't put your spouse down for suggesting it. Always validate their suggestion as a possibility, explain why you disagree, and then ask for their assistance in coming up with "something both of us might like."

DON'T carry on when your spouse's answer is *no*. A no is rarely final and usually serves to mark the real starting point of the negotiation process.

DON'T talk when your partner is talking. You can't negotiate with anyone until you know what they're thinking, and you can't know what they're thinking until you listen to them. Always allow your spouse to speak more than you do.

Knowledge speaks. Wisdom listens.

To listen effectively, we also must learn to contend with the Grand Central Station traffic which is arriving and departing simultaneously on every track in our mind.

When talking to others, we actually hear two voices. We hear the person who is speaking, and we hear our own inner voice. The inner voice is the one that follows everything that is said and then formulates our desired responses. The responses are manufactured almost simultaneously with what is heard. They track the incoming comments like an instantaneous stock market ticker tape.

We can think two-and-a-half to three times faster than our spouse can speak. This gives us ample time to listen effectively and then prepare our responses. We have the time to do both. But most of us just focus on the preparing responses part.

Try to block out your typical listening thoughts. Realign your internal voice toward learning your partner's position rather than automatically resisting it. To let your spouse know you were, indeed, listening to them, wait that three seconds before responding, and then consider using one of these openers:

- So, to be sure I understand, your preference is _____. Is that correct?

- When I made that remark, it made you feel _____. Am I describing this correctly?

- I think I hear you; your biggest concern is _____. Do I have it right?

Despite your best efforts, be warned that the odds are high your spouse will still hear something you did not say. Remember, they are also listening to their internal voice. This is why you should not get angry at your partner's response when you first hear it. The likelihood is they are talking about something that exists in their mind only. Try to determine what your spouse heard you say. It is vital that you know what they think you said.

Our saying it does not mean they understand it.

Hear-Say

Experts tell us that only about 25 percent of what we say will actually register with our listeners. This fact alone is surprising, but the real shocker is that we also say only a portion of what we think we said.

Experts claim to have recorded their own phone conversations, then later confirmed there was a remarkable difference between what they thought they said and what they, in fact, did say.

In other words, we cannot hear everything *we* say, much less what *they* say. There is too much going on in our heads.

This same interference is blasted back and forth even in our normal day-to-day conversations. Toss in the static that comes with divorce – stressors like anxiety, anger, etc. – and we finally catch a solid glimpse of how hard it is to achieve a meeting of the minds. No wonder we need help trying to make sense to our spouse.

An Ear for an Ear
It is highly recommended that we repeat our spouse's concerns and their settlement thoughts back to them. This lets them know that we did, in fact, hear what they said. But it also clears their mind so they can listen to us.

Otherwise, when it is our turn to talk, they are likely to be half-listening to us and half-listening to the crossfire going on in their head. Their inner mind will be clicking at Mach 3, trying to create another presentation of what they think just went over our head.

Keep listening until you understand your spouse's concerns well enough to repeat them right back – the more verbatim the better. Then, and only then, can you reasonably expect your spouse to have the willingness to listen to what you have to say.

When you are paraphrasing your partner's message, your partner still has the floor. If you want them to acknowledge your point of view, acknowledge theirs first. If you want your spouse to stop making the same argument over and over again, simply acknowledge that you heard them. You do that by repeating their words back to them.

If the two of you keep going around and around in some sort of verbal cul-de-sac, it means that someone is not listening.

Hear and now.

Hearing Aids
Words – language and listening – are the tools available to us as we try to reach a divorce settlement. But, like all tools, they must be used correctly or they'll do more damage than good.

This is why two of the major components of the "nice approach" are directly related to the words we say and hear:

- Listen to what your spouse says, convince them you heard every word they said, and, know what to say and when to say it.
- Then say it nicely.

No one is going to have a change of mind based on what someone is barking at them. But, if you can get your spouse to vent properly, their thinking can become moldable. When painful feelings are expressed, the pain lessens and progress becomes possible.

Try to show curiosity about your partner's position because it verifies you were listening and that you are trying to understand their side. It also makes you look less critical, less judgmental, and less controlling. Humans become easier to deal with when their beliefs are not instantly shot down.

If you and your spouse reach a disagreement on a particular point, it can be helpful to say, "Okay, so we have a disagreement. The way I see it, the disagreement is . . ." or "Do you see it the same way? I'm for putting it on the shelf for a while and coming back to it later, after we make some progress on other issues. Is this agreeable?"

People desperately need understanding from their counterparts in conflict. (Remember Chapter 2, when we noted there is a basic human need to be understood?) Be understanding. It costs you nothing, and you stand to gain everything.

Please take note of the following:

1. **Understand that no one changes their mind until they have been heard and until they *know* they have been heard.**

    - Show that you want to understand your spouse's position by asking supporting questions.
    - Remember that listening can change both the speaker and the listener.
    - Know that your partner won't listen until you have first given them a reason to listen.
    - Remember that reciprocal listening helps to change minds.
    - Recognize that listening is your red carpet to reestablishing trust.

2. **Try to listen with the intent to understand your spouse's point of view.**

    - Try to get into your partner's world.
    - Hear between the lines.
    - Catch the flow of what they are saying and ride along with it.
    - Repeat their words back to them, maintaining their point of view, not your own.
    - Realize that in order to persuade, you must first transmit the belief that you are open to persuasion.
    - Assume, or at least pretend, there is a lot to learn from what your spouse has to say.

3. **Use positive visual cues to indicate you are listening to your spouse.**

    - Facial expression and eye contact are two important visual clues. If you avoid eye contact while listening, you will likely communicate disapproval or lack of interest.
    - Try to assume the most "listening" position you can. Uncross your hands and legs, sit up straight on the edge of the seat, face the speaker, and lean forward. And, of course, maintain eye contact.
    - Be careful your facial expression does not indicate negativity.

        The cues that reap the most benefits are a combination of a smiling face with direct eye contact. Add an occasional head nod to this mix, and you transmit a nonjudgmental and caring confirmation of what your spouse is saying.

        Our nonverbal cues include posture, facial expressions, hand gestures, eye movement and contact, personal space, and voice inflection.

Body language speaks the loudest.

Not listening to our spouse is the heart disease of divorce negotiations.

Now what?

We have now explored the three basics that influence our spousal divorce settlement discussions – perspective, emotions, and language/listening.

But I want you to know more than the fundamentals of the buddy approach. The rest of the book is going to take you through every possible negotiation obstacle, situation, curveball, and trip wire.

Chapter 10
The Obstacle Course – Nine Invisible Hurdles & How To Jump Them

The material we've covered so far will get us around the tip of the negotiation iceberg, but we cannot afford to overlook the really scary part: the 90 percent that lurks beneath the surface.

There, unseen, are the obstacles that we should be looking for. Some are everyday, common sense items that we are already somewhat familiar with; but few of us seem to understand how truly destructive they can be. Without being forewarned, we normally tend to brush them off and minimize their impact.

Here they are, along with instructions for handling them.

One Spouse Wants a Divorce, One Doesn't

The Obstacle

At the beginning of a divorce case, one spouse is usually more motivated to end the marriage than the other one is. This causes a problem within a problem. Divorce is difficult enough when both parties agree that it's time, but having both parties at odds about getting a divorce creates another level of conflict. It automatically has a drastic effect on any hopes for an early resolution.

The announcement of a divorce often causes trauma to the less-motivated spouse. This forestalls their willingness to discuss settlement and hurts the motivated spouse's chances for an early resolution. It is wise if the motivated spouse does not push for a settlement before the other party has had ample time to come to grips with getting divorced.

More often than not, the one who wants the divorce will grow impatient and become less tolerant of the other's reluctance. They begin to resent the other party for dragging their feet or perhaps overplaying the trauma card, and this attitude complicates and inflames everything. It never pays to rattle someone who has power over us. And make no mistake, if the goal is to settle out of court, the spouse who wants the divorce the *least* is the one with all the power.

To make things even worse, the less-motivated spouses often tend to stall for time even after their emotional blockage has subsided. Some do this when their initial hurt turns into anger, some do it to enhance their bargaining position, and some do it just to make it hard for the other party.

Jumping the Hurdle

If your partner doesn't want a divorce and you do, and you want to make your divorce less agonizing and costly, you have no viable alternative but to wait it out. We jump this hurdle by knowing *how* to wait it out.

We do this by accepting that:

- The negotiation process is only as quick as the pace of its slowest participant, and that our partner's pace is out of our control.
- Our spouse's willingness to negotiate is not something we can speed up. It comes with the passage of time.
- We must never push our spouse.

- We must tolerate their foot dragging for as long as we can. Complaining about it creates more delay than the reluctance itself.
- We must be patient or appear to be patient.
- We must never let our spouse see how much their pokiness irritates us.
- We are hurting ourselves (or at least wasting our breath) if we begin negotiations before our spouse is emotionally up to it.

Take This Deal and Love It

The Obstacle

Even when both spouses are willing to discuss settlement, their varying styles can be problematic.

All decisions concerning a divorce are big decisions, and big decisions take time. They cannot be hurried, and it is naïve to expect otherwise. Just as water seeks its own level, we make decisions at our own level. One spouse's timetable cannot rule over the other spouse's timetable.

We process big decisions by systematically becoming familiar with the product (e.g., we seldom buy the first home we inspect, nor do we buy the first auto we see). It takes time to get comfortable with making a big move. This is true even if we actually want the item, but divorce requires more processing because it is not something we want – at least not in the same way we want a home or car.

Our individual comfort zone tells us when to make a decision. If that is threatened, we will take the path of least resistance. We will kick into our default mode and say no.

Delays may also occur if the parties have different personality types. For example, extroverts need less time to size up a situation than introverts need. Some individuals are impulsive by nature, while others are more deliberate and prone to indecision. We must allow for these style differences or we are likely to get a premature no.

In addition, the financially dependent spouse may need extra time to grasp the money aspect of divorce or to get a more comfortable understanding of their financial future. We all resent being rushed, we resent sales pressure, and we try to squirm away from both. Aside from annoying us or making us uncomfortable, these tactics also trigger distrust. If we lose trust, we say no or we stall until it becomes less awkward for us to say no.

Another aspect of this obstacle deserves special recognition. Simply put, we categorically reject generous settlement offers that are made during the beginning stages of conflict. When we receive such an offer, we freeze as if someone just hit the pause button. If our mind was a physical object that we could observe, and if we could see it at that precise moment, our reaction would be just like that of a deer in headlights.

I don't think we react this way because of skepticism regarding the value of the offer or because of our ego or pride or our fear of being a sucker. I think it is simply what happens when something comes at us out of the blue. Asking a person to accept a particular deal, when they may not be prepared to discuss any deal at all, definitely falls into this category.

If your generous offer is made too early, expect to receive a cold response. It is not about how good the deal is or isn't. It is probably because of that big pause button in the sky.

Jumping the Hurdle

We must create a negotiation climate in which our spouse does not feel pressured or rushed. We must be patient and allow our partner to *be* a partner, with a sense of shared control and ownership in the proceedings.

There are specific things we can say, right up front, that will help create a climate of cooperation:

- I know that we will reach a settlement, but I want you to know that I won't be happy with anything we agree on unless you are just as happy as I am.

- I want our mutual satisfaction to be our real target. If we get off track, I give you permission to remind me of this, and I hope you will allow me to do the same.

There are also specific things we can do to help maintain a cooperative climate:

DO proceed at your spouse's pace, not yours.

DO try to put your own needs aside momentarily and imagine yourself in your spouse's reality.

DO keep an open mind. You never know when you or your spouse may say something that you can use later as a stepping-stone to a settlement.

You Won't Find Feelings on a Spreadsheet

The Obstacle
Conversations between spouses concerning a divorce settlement are not as much about dollars as they first seem. They sound like they are about money, but they are really about unresolved feelings, which do not appear on a spreadsheet.

Feelings are a big part of divorce negotiations, and we must neutralize them before we can expect our negotiations to be productive. Unresolved feelings cause us to dwell on the problem instead of on the solution, and the longer we do this, the longer our divorce will take.

Feelings aren't right or wrong; they just are.

Talking settlement without talking about feelings is like trying to float a boat without water. We will never be pleased with a settlement agreement unless we vent all of our grievances before entering into it. Any immediate sense of relief we get from settling without venting is not worth the longer-lasting regret that follows.

This is another reason to tolerate our spouse's flak; it plays a large part in getting them to surrender.

Jumping the Hurdle
One way to neutralize our feelings is to talk about them objectively. Talking about the emotions that you are experiencing will lessen the

negative effect of those emotions. Here are some examples of neutralizing statements:

- I don't know about you, but I'm feeling frustrated at how long this is taking.

- I am having difficulty controlling my anger. I hope that this isn't making things harder for you.

Emotions have been touched on in greater detail in Chapter 8, but here are a few refreshers important when confronting this obstacle:

DON'T ever say you know how your spouse feels. This is the ultimate no-no. Your spouse always has the final word on what they are feeling.

However, it is helpful to comment on the emotion they are displaying (e.g., "You seem angry").

It is important that you try to identify the emotion and then mention it, and it will not hurt things if you identify the wrong emotion. Experts advise that it is therapeutic for your partner to sense that you have picked up on their agony, no matter what name tag you give it.

And – remember – your spouse has the final word on what they are feeling.

DON'T expect sympathy from your spouse. Your spouse definitely expects to get sympathy from you, not the other way around.

DON'T insult your partner. Insults, blunt or masked, will hurt your case.

A blunt example is, "I'm a slob? Maybe I'm not a slob. Maybe it's just that you are an anal, compulsive neat freak."

A masked insult is, "It's easy to see why you feel justified in slamming the phone down on my friends. Where do they get off thinking you're a hothead?"

DON'T react when your spouse throws a zinger at you. Deal with it by turning the zinger into a question, such as, "I am sincerely curious about why you feel that I'm the cause of the breakdown in our communications. Sometimes I don't see the whole picture, so please tell me where you feel I went wrong."

DON'T say things like "Calm down" or "You're over-reacting."

These are word grenades, as are the following:

Get a grip.
Get over it.
Grow up.
Anyone see my violin?
Looks like someone got up on the wrong side of the bed today.
What's eating you today?
Surely you're joking.
My heart bleeds for you.

You Started It

The Obstacle
Our historic inability to settle our own divorces is based, in large part, on the fact that we can't resist injecting blame or fault into the negotiations.

Do not blame your spouse for anything.
Blame just makes them angry, and angry people don't settle.

No one wants to accept that they have been "bad." Think of when you were a child and got caught fighting with a sibling. Does "He started it" sound familiar? Blame will cause your spouse to shut down. Then you will never be heard.

Our tendency to blame is hazardous to our wealth. The smart money focuses on problem solving instead of blame placing. Blaming is also senseless because no one on this planet is ever wrong. It's *always* the other guy. Everyone, in every conflict, finds a way of exonerating themselves. If humanity had a universal mantra, it would be *"I'm innocent; it's their fault."*

Your job is not to build a case to prove your partner is a rat or that you're right and your partner is wrong. You can stay married to do that or you can vent with your friends and family. Your job now is to save time, money, and pain; and blaming hinders all three. Build the bridge; don't blow it up.

Get their signature today; you can always be right tomorrow.

Blame fixes nothing and is totally useless. Here's an example of how useless it is.

Let's say you are stopped at a traffic light on a busy highway and get hit in the rear by a drunk driver. Your car sustains major damage and blocks traffic in both directions. A tow truck finally arrives after 90 minutes of incessant honking from the other motorists. Instead of immediately arranging to have your vehicle moved to the shoulder, you repeatedly complain to the tow operator about how innocent you are and how guilty the other driver is.

You can blame all day long, but it won't move your car, and it won't stop the honking.

Jumping the Hurdle

The main thing to keep in mind is this: don't beat your spouse over the head about something that happened in the past. Keep your focus on the future and not on what occurred months or years ago. The past is what brought you into conflict. Talking about it now only prolongs the conflict.

Remember, no one has ever changed history by complaining about it.

Dwelling on the past does as much good as burning down your house to kill a mouse. So, don't criticize your spouse about the past. Forget about their shortcomings as a companion, parent, homemaker, breadwinner, etc. Instead, remember that everything that drives you crazy about your spouse is what you are leaving behind. No matter how justified your complaints may be, your spouse doesn't get it and never will.

And it serves no purpose to discuss past deeds with someone who doesn't get it.

Divorce Papers Are Scary

The Obstacle

The mere involvement of the legal system will often cause unanticipated delays. I have yet to meet a person who took kindly to divorce papers filed by their spouse, no matter how "no-fault" the papers sounded. We do not like reading about our lives in court documents.

Divorce papers are formal, no-nonsense, and downright scary. A divorce case is still a legal case, and the law requires lawyers to meet certain standards of pleading even when their clients would prefer they refrain from riling up the other side. Lawyers have little choice in the matter. Court papers are court papers, friendly divorce or not. Even the most softened documents are humbling and brutal to the spouse who receives them.

Divorce papers also convey a sense of powerlessness, not unlike the feeling we get when a traffic cop reminds us we are not free to roam the countryside at any speed we wish. They let us know our civil rights have changed and that we can now be put under house arrest. The papers tell us that the legal system has taken away our keys to run our own lives – that the court is now empowered to dole out the constitutional rights (to freedom, movement, speech, property, privacy, etc.) that we may exercise during the time our case is pending.

Jumping the Hurdle

It is important that the party against whom the case is filed does not overreact. If appropriate, they should be told that the act of filing is typically more mechanical than it is meaningful. It also helps to explain that the wording in the papers is likely to be the same boilerplate language that lawyers use in every case, and that the affected spouse was not singled out.

The legal system creates enough fear and anxiety as it is; the mere act of filing should not be allowed to unnecessarily add to the havoc.

You Can't Spend a Pound of Flesh

The Obstacle

Another delay surfaces when one of the parties feels wronged or angry. They are the "victim," and they want the court to know it. These spouses don't care if the case takes a long time; they just want the judge to know how bad their partner is. They count on the judge sharing their outrage and making the other party suffer, but this is just wishful thinking on their part. This behavior doesn't help them in court. All it does is make it harder for the other party to get them to settle. This costs everyone more money and frustration.

The worst place in the world to seek revenge is in the legal system.

Trying to get revenge costs too much, takes too long, and usually hurts us just as much as it hurts the person we want to hurt. It is like stabbing ourselves through the stomach with a sword in order to inflict pain on the guy standing in line behind us.

Most aggrieved partners do not take kindly to the fact that the court cannot consider misconduct as a factor in determining monetary or property awards. The judge is not going to declare who the victim is, and then torture the wrongdoer spouse in the town square for all the neighbors to see.

Divorce is where the guilty go free.

It is asking a lot to expect an early settlement if one of the parties persists in entertaining unrealistic, though perhaps understandable, expectations about what the legal system will actually do for them. It's much too easy to be misled by Hollywood and a generation or two of TV lawyer shows that depict justice as being instantaneous and sure – you know, where the bad guy always gets what's coming to him and the good guy gets to walk off into the sunset, ready to do it all again next week. Real life doesn't work like this.

The judge cannot compensate you for your spouse's bad behavior. Most people entering divorce proceedings want their day in court because they want the judge to mete out the justice that their spouse has long withheld. You deserve it, right? Right. And yet our court system is not designed to give it to you!

As explained in Chapter 2, our divorce courts follow only the facts and the law. They do not take our hurt feelings or need for vengeance into account.

Jumping the Hurdle

Start by accepting that there is no back pay in divorce for your partner's misdeeds. The system will not magically provide you with compensation because your spouse is a louse, so focus on the future by not making these mistakes in the present:

> **DON'T** make statements blaming your spouse for the past because you feel victimized (see Obstacle 4).

> **DON'T** display a "you owe me" attitude or make any statements that depict you as a victim. Statements such as "I've given you my best years, and now, because of you and your tootsie, I'm probably going to end up being a bag lady" will only anger your spouse and won't help your cause one bit.

> **DON'T** transmit that you believe you should receive something extra because of past deeds. Things like working a lot of overtime or two jobs, cooking, cleaning, supporting the other's career, etc., simply do not count. There is no back pay.

Incoming! Incoming!

The Obstacle

We have not yet learned the importance of handling our spouse's aggression. If we know how to prepare for this, we have a good chance of neutralizing its effect.

How do we brace ourselves for this? We do it simply by expecting it. If you expect your spouse to cross the line, then you are prepared to handle it when they do.

A barrage of fury usually awaits all of us at the bargaining table. This is predictable. We should not be concerned about what our spouse says or does; how we respond to what's said and done is what should be important to us.

We should accept our spouse's behavior as the first part of a dance that will lead us to settlement. It is better for your partner to blow off now rather than in the corridor in front of the courtroom.

We seem to feel that bracing ourselves for an onslaught is optional, when, in actuality, it is of paramount importance. Don't take your spouse's confrontational behavior personally. Instead, see it as a mere part of the whole settlement picture. It provides an excellent opportunity to show off your newfound poise. Welcome it.

We must anticipate some grief from our spouse and not allow ourselves to get bent out of shape when things start flying. Boxers do not flip out when they take a few punches; they expect it. The same is true when football players are tackled; it is part of the game.

It is, however, also very important that we do not underestimate how bad the aggression will be. We must expect the worst blast imaginable or we will instinctively respond with all the nastiness at our command. This reaction, of course, will cause the very delays that we are seeking to avoid.

Our goal is to dismantle our spouse's anger because angry people do not make deals. They fight.

Competitors in other endeavors know the importance of preparing for their event, so why don't we? The stakes in our contest are hardly unimportant; they involve our house, our kids, our pocketbooks, and our future. What makes us think we can just wing it and say whatever pops into our head? The answer is we cannot, and our expensive, overcrowded legal system proves this.

Jumping the Hurdle

> **DO** be very careful of your first reaction. Anticipate that you will hear something that will infuriate you and be ready to deliver a non-offensive response.
>
> **DON'T** be confrontational. Forget saying things like, "That's not what happened and you know it" or "Maybe

you should have thought of that before you took up with your boss" or "I'll go to jail first before I . . ."

Equally bad are confrontational questions such as, "Why are you being so emotional?" or "Why are you doing this to me?" Instead say things like, "Tell me more," and "Please help me to understand."

DON'T attack your spouse. Instead, attack the problem *with* your spouse. For example, say, "The problem really isn't because of you or me. It's because there isn't enough money to go around. Let's see what we can do to make the shoe fit."

DON'T respond with angry threats. Don't say, "I'll quit my job, and then what'll you have?" or "I'm going for full custody" or "That's it, I'm through talking to you. I'm hiring a Doberman for a lawyer and you're going to regret the day…"

Cogito, Ergo Sue 'em

The Obstacle

I think, therefore I am *[right]*.

Divorcing spouses do not see problems in the same way. In fact, they are usually arguing about two different things without realizing it. If they saw the underlying facts of their controversy in the same way, they probably wouldn't be in conflict to begin with.

Here's another way of saying it: most disputers think they are in conflict because they cannot agree on a solution. What they fail to realize is that the conflict exists because they cannot agree on the problem.

An example: Husband wants more romance in the marriage and talks to Wife about his feelings. Wife responds by saying that Husband never helps her out around the house and he watches too much television.

Husband thinks the conflict is about the frequency of their intimacy. Wife thinks the conflict is about Husband's laziness and lack of appreciation for all she does. Doesn't he understand that she also would like to watch television? Instead, she works herself into near exhaustion, and her reward is to hear him ask for more pleasure in his already soft life.

If you gave truth serum to each of them, Husband would say that Wife was making too much of his so-called laziness and that laziness really has nothing to do with intimacy. He is resentful because she has grown indifferent to his needs.

Wife would say that Husband cannot reasonably expect her to be more amorous when she barely has enough time to brush her teeth. She is resentful because he is not appreciative of her sacrifices. She develops a belief that he is the one who has become indifferent.

Husband's "logic" fits the facts that only he sees. This "logic" is lost on Wife because she sees an entirely different set of facts (which are unknown to Husband). Likewise, Wife (who does not know that Husband sees different facts) bases her "logic" on facts that only she sees.

We apply our thinking to a solution using facts that do not exist in the other party's mind. One party's "logic" can only be persuasive to someone who sees the facts in the same way that that party does. Needless to say, this does not occur as often as we need it to.

Jumping the Hurdle

Instead of getting angry when our partner says no to our well-reasoned offer, we must remember that there is "more than one no." In other words, their *no* may not be in response to the way *we* see things. More likely, it is in response to how *they* see things.

Before reacting, we have to find out what facts our spouse is addressing. Only then can we understand why they have given us a no.

Ask yourself two questions:

1. What do they understand the underlying facts of the controversy to be?

2. Would their *no* be an acceptable answer to the set of facts that they are seeing?

Do not see their *no* as the end. See it as a sign that you have some more work to do.

Trust or Consequences

The Obstacle

Another large impediment that presents itself during divorce discussions is lack of trust. Losing trust during divorce is quite common and normally begins when the spouses first start to pull away from one another.

Trust disappears overnight and does not announce its departure. It is one of the first things to go, because the multitude of negative feelings that accompany divorce promptly overrides any sense of trust that was established during the marriage.

The person you married did trust you, true. This new person does not. Accept this as a fact and don't debate it. You and your partner are not exceptions to this reality of divorce.

Let's face it: divorce is anti-trust. Your soon-to-be ex now has the natural right to be skeptical about you and anything you say. You are now the enemy. Expecting your soon-to-be ex to trust you is about as realistic as thinking you can kick-start Air Force One.

Trust is a vital ingredient to successful negotiation. With trust, deals get done quicker and easier. Never minimize the impact that its loss will bring to the bargaining table.

Jumping the Hurdle

It helps to build your partner's distrust into your thinking. Lack of trust may account for their new attitude or for their sudden defiance or unyielding tone of voice. It is easier to tolerate this unexpected behavior when we know why it is happening.

We must do whatever we can to insure that our ability to persuade is not trampled by our spouse's newly developed, but seldom announced, instinct to reject our persuasion. We must especially prove ourselves trustworthy in every step of the settlement process. We cannot give our partner any new reasons to buttress their distrust.

Whew!

We've done it…jumped the nine hurdles of the divorce obstacle course, one by one. We now have seen it all, right? Right.

The truth is, even though each obstacle is deadly all on its own, we rarely find just one doing all the damage. They intertwine like fiber optic wiring within a phone cable.

As soon as we finish the last of the obstacles – the eleven specific situations and curveballs – you'll be prepared for all the lethal combinations that might come your way.

Speaking of curveballs…

Chapter 11
What to Do When –
Eleven Specific Situations & Curveballs

In this chapter, we'll round off obstacles by looking at eleven specific situations and curveballs, and help you understand "what to do when . . ."

1: Who Should Make the First Offer?
Conventional wisdom has always warned against being the one to make the first offer during divorce negotiations, strongly advising that we wait for the other side to go first. This point of view insists that the party making the first offer rings a bell that can never be un-rung, that it shortens the playing field, and that it sets a limit on the best deal the offer-making party can ever expect to receive.

However, there are now *two* professionally accepted schools of thought regarding the advisability of making the first offer.

Damned if you do and damned if your spouse does it first.

On the other side of the conventional wisdom coin, a number of top negotiators now believe that the party making the first offer actually gains a superior bargaining position. They feel the first offer indicates strength and confidence and anchors the settlement talks in the offer-making party's chosen bargaining zone.

I favor going first. My personal experience tells me it works better, and it is a more comfortable fit for me.

Both schools of thought recommend that the parties try to delay getting to the first-offer stage. If the big demands begin too early, the walls of defense start going up prematurely and are likely to snuff out the interchange that is usually needed to serve as a foundation for the big demands.

If you do make the first offer, it is best to preface it with a polite statement about the legal standard that governs the situation. State your understanding of the law or other applicable standard that would normally apply in your situation, and then diplomatically guide them to your position. Meet them, and then lead them.

For example, say something like, "My understanding of the law is that in cases involving a marriage of over twenty-five years, where the 'breadwinner' spouse is expected always to earn considerably more than the 'homemaker' spouse, maintenance (alimony) is normally awarded on a permanent basis. With this in mind, I believe that maintenance in our case should be long-term and should not end in five years, as I believe was mentioned earlier."

If your spouse doesn't agree, follow with questions like these: "Am I missing something?" or "Is there another standard I am not familiar with?" or "If I am off-base, please show me where I am off-base."

Here's some more advice for when you make the first offer:

> **DON'T** ask for something outrageous unless you find joy in paying outrageous attorney's fees. Divorce wars don't pay; you do.
>
> **DON'T** shoot from the hip or say what comes naturally. This is one of the times in life that we do *not* have free speech.
>
> **DON'T** start at your bottom line. Inexperienced negotiators feel more comfortable doing so, but try to resist this temptation because it leaves no room for compro-

mise. It leads to deadlock, and deadlock leads to a court battle.

DON'T start tough and refuse to budge.

DON'T start in the middle and refuse to budge. Create negotiating room by starting somewhere between the middle and your dream result. Then move in small increments that always get smaller.

DON'T ever add "value" (real or imagined) to your offer. Remarks like, "Anyone in their right mind would know that I am being way too generous" convey your superiority and imply that your spouse is stupid for not knowing what is "good" for them.

Always indicate flexibility in your price and state a non-argumentative reason for your position, especially when you are asking for more than your spouse has in mind. For example, try making a statement such as, "I'm not saying my number is carved in stone, but I think it is very close to how the judge will rule. I could be wrong, but this is my honest belief."

Whenever possible, avoid speaking in dollars and cents. In fact, don't say the word *dollars*. For example, don't say, "I'll give you 35,000 dollars." Instead say, "35,000 is reasonable."

If your spouse acts surprised at your offer, act surprised at their surprise, and then ask if you've said something to offend them. And try not to react if you make an offer and your spouse winces. Merely keep your calm and repeat the offer. You could also ask them in a friendly fashion what they were expecting. Use their response to further the negotiation process.

Now, what do you do if your spouse makes the first offer?

DO flinch or react with mild surprise when they make a proposal. They are watching for your reaction. A flinch indicates you can't (not won't) accept their proposal. It is a polite way of indicating your disapproval. People believe what they see more than what they hear. You can usually expect a softening or a concession after a credible flinch.

DON'T say yes to a first offer, even if you think it's a good deal. Doing so leaves the other spouse with thoughts that they offered too much. You want your partner to feel good about the negotiations and not be kicking themselves later. They will always be a part of your life, and you don't want your ex harboring angry feelings about not getting a better deal.

DON'T say no too quickly. Allow sufficient time to pass before you respond. If you want your spouse to give serious thought to what you want, you have to give at least the impression of giving serious thought to what your spouse wants.

2: When Your Spouse Pushes for a Ball Park Number (Or, What's Behind Curtain #3?)

Everyone wants to know the answer to everything right now. At the same time, we are naturally hesitant to reveal our real thoughts because we don't want to be held to any position until we have had a chance to really think it through.

So, when other side pushes and says something like, "Give me a ballpark so I at least have some idea where this is headed."

Do *not* give them a ballpark.

Tell them you need more time to think about it. To mention a ballpark number is to lock yourself in, and it gives them a chance to start whittling you down, right on the spot. Dodging the question will cause you some discomfort, but it beats addressing a dead-end question.

3: Leave Haggling to the Hagglers

Be careful. Making the first offer too soon (#1 above) or being forced into ball-parking a settlement figure too early (#2) can lead to haggling. This should be avoided at all costs.

Haggling is what you see in movie scenes that depict how things are done in third world street markets. If haggling worked in divorce, our courts wouldn't be standing room only.

Haggling is overwhelming. It does nothing more than stimulate doubt and second-guessing, neither of which does anything positive to satisfy either party. Again, some degree of satisfaction is essential in divorce negotiations, and this can only happen if both partners vent freely before tackling the larger issues and feel they were heard and validated.

Haggling does not provide such a benefit, because haggling is not negotiating. Haggling is just . . . haggling.

Remember, you will probably have to deal with your spouse again, and you don't want them dissatisfied and gunning for you.

4: Does the First One to Speak Always Lose?

Car salespersons have bragged for years that, after they offer a deal to a customer, they will intentionally remain silent. They wait to see who speaks first: the customer or them. And they fully intend it to be the customer.

Their philosophy is that the party who speaks first loses because speaking first is believed to be a sign of surrender. So, if the customer speaks first, the salesperson can hang tough on the last price mentioned. If the salesperson slips and speaks first, then the price comes down and the customer gets a better deal.

The silence is terribly uncomfortable, and the party who is unaccustomed to it will want to speak, just to end the discomfort. The salesperson, of course, will have no discomfort. They do this every day and can sit in silence for hours if need be.

However, here's a technique to use if your spouse tries this on you: break the silence by saying, "What would you do if you were in my shoes?"

The spell is usually broken if the first one to speak asks a question.

5: Or Else What? When Your Spouse Gives an Ultimatum

And here comes the ultimatum. They say, "Take it or leave it. This is my final offer." How should we respond?

The best thing to do is to ignore the statement and go on as if it never existed. Never, ever mention or allude to it. Just keep talking and allow it to fade into oblivion.

Don't take the ultimatum personally and fire back. Most ultimatums are blurted out in moments of frustration and are short-lived, most evaporate naturally and quickly. Ignoring an ultimatum gives your partner the unspoken opportunity to continue the negotiations without loss of face.

When they say you must settle by a certain date or time, ask, "What if I take a little more time but I come back with a counterproposal that gives you just as good a deal? Would that be okay?"

Or, if your spouse insists you accept their proposal here and now "or else," you can subdue the urgency by asking, "How about if I give it some thought and come up with something even better? That's okay too, isn't it?"

These types of questions calm the situation instead of aggravating it.

Another way to handle an ultimatum is to tell them, "You know, I might go along with this if you would agree to some of the other things I've asked for." When they ask what those are, tell them you want to be very careful before presenting them, and that you would like a day or so to state them properly.

This is not about bargaining for extra time. Asking these questions neutralizes the threat and gives them a chance to get off the hook for making the threat.

6: When Your Spouse Pushes for an Answer

If your spouse seems insistent on getting you to agree to a major item that you are not ready to give away, do not let it become a sticking point.

Neutralize the problem by asking this question: "What if [this big thing you want from me] was not a problem? Where would we stand then?" This should alter the flow and move the spotlight from the major issue. If it doesn't, ask to shelve it until some of the smaller things have been resolved.

This response should prevent a delicate issue from causing a premature deadlock. You can always revisit the major item later, but it will no longer be a do-or-die item.

7: Is That a Threat?

A sure way to push your spouse into a courtroom battle is to ask them for a yes-or-no answer. For example, "Did you refuse to be nice to my family or not?" or "Did you make the $800 withdrawal or not?"

This kind of question is usually followed by, "Just answer yes or no. Did you or didn't you?"

This may work in a courtroom *after* a war has begun, but it does little to avoid the war itself. It is belligerent and has no place in divorce settlement conversations.

In fact, "Did you or didn't you" is only second in counter-productivity to the question that I find to be downright laughable. This #1 question is the infamous, "Is that a threat?"

I think this first surfaced in a 1930s movie and has very little, if any, legal significance. Apparently a non-lawyer screenwriter mistakenly attached a "profound" end-all meaning to it, and those that don't know better continue to use it to this day.

If you hear it in your divorce discussions, overcome the temptation to snap back. Instead, try to ignore it by switching the conversation to something else.

If you are not comfortable doing this, then fire "Is *that* a threat?" right back at them. It is as absurd as their question; it should shut them up long enough for you to restore sanity in the room. Do this by saying "Okay, you win; we're even! I threatened, you threatened, and now we're almost back to where we started. I was hoping we could make some decent progress today. I'm willing to try and I hope you are, too. I say, let's get back to figuring out something that works for both of us."

8: When Your Spouse Heads for the Door

When your spouse is through talking and starts heading for the door, calmly state, "If you are intent on giving up and taking this to court, then please take this with you and think about it."

Scribble a quick offer on a piece of paper and hand it to them. Limit the offer to only the biggest issue (because that is usually all you will have time to write) and tell them it is not to be opened until later.

This may seem like a long shot, last ditch attempt to settle your divorce, but it is really a disguised last ditch attempt to keep your settlement chances alive. If your spouse is done negotiating, so be it. But, if there is some glimmer of hope for reviving settlement discussions, the note gives your spouse a face-saving way of returning to the table.

9: Speaking to the Devil – Negotiation Bullies

"Negotiation bullies" is my term for spouses who are exceptionally forceful or belligerent – you know, the kind that were born mean and weaned on vinegar.

As we already discussed in Chapter 5, the essence of the buddy system settlement approach – **Act nicely toward your spouse, no matter what** – does not work in cases where your spouse is a bully or is otherwise handicapped when it comes to compromising.

Remember, I define a "reasonable spouse" as one who is able to understand (but not necessarily agree with) how the other side justifies their settlement position. Many people are not able to do this, and this is why we have wars. There is simply no talking to some people.

Bullies are not built to be fair. It is like asking them to fly. It is impossible to reason with them, because they are only able to see their side of the argument. There is no gray in their world, because they do not comprehend that there may be another way of seeing things. They are negotiation sociopaths.

Most spouses who give in to bullies find some initial relief, but later regret doing so. Bullies do not budge during the talking stage of a case, so any negotiations prior to the morning of trial are usually fruitless. They will not show their first sign of "reasonableness" until minutes before trial is to start and, even then, they don't negotiate. They haggle.

Never haggle with a bully, because they are too good at it.

And they know it. Haggling is the closest they can come to negotiating.

A bully has a way of transmitting superiority in negotiations even when there is no realistic basis for doing so. They still need you to say yes in order to get their way, and that makes you just as "superior."

Psychologists have discovered that one of the biggest reasons we tend to let bullies get the better of us is because most of us have a natural desire to avoid conflict whenever we can. A bully senses this "weakness," and their predatory instincts take over.

Know yourself and, if you believe a bully would normally overpower you, hire a good lawyer to do the talking for you.

There is no shame in not beating a bully at their own game. Some of us are taller, some of us are diabetic, some of us need eyeglasses, and some of us are bullies. This is just the way it is. It certainly doesn't make the bully a better person than you; it just means that you probably have more friends. Bullies don't have friends – only followers.

If it turns out you do wind up settling with a bully, do not give your formal yes for a minimum of twenty-four hours. Think about it overnight.

If your spouse is not a bully, but is just an extremely competitive person, resist the temptation to challenge them directly. Unlike bullies, they can be as reasonable as the rest of humanity; but you don't want to stir up their competitive spirit. Package your resistance subtly and diplomatically. It is unwise to openly compete with a competitor if you hope to cut your costs or your pain.

Our divorce court system isn't perfect, but it will treat you better than a bully will.

10: Negotiating via E-mail and Telephone
Don't do it.

Divorce negotiations are delicate, and they require all the warmth and sincerity we can transmit. Face-to-face conversations provide us with our best opportunity to get our spouse to hear our side.

Communication experts believe that our words convey only 10 percent of what we say, and that the other 90 percent is communicated through our body language, eyes, facial expressions, and voice inflections. These are our best persuasion tools, and it is foolish for us not to use them whenever possible.

With this in mind, e-mail is the same as sending a telegram, and negotiating over the telephone isn't much better.

The telephone, at least, does allow for some of our vocal tone variations. Without the eye contact and gestures, however, their effectiveness is likely to evaporate mid-wire before it can get to your partner's ears.

If you have no choice but to do some of your negotiating over the telephone, try to be as upbeat as you can. Schedule the calls for times of the day when both of you are typically less harried and more likely to be in a decent mood.

Neither you nor your partner should ever be on the phone if it's a bad day, a bad time of the day, if either of you is in a bad mood or if any interruptions are anticipated.

Aside from giving our spouse two additional ways to misinterpret our message, there is another problem with e-mailing and telephoning. It is easier for the opposition to become snotty when we are not face-to-face with them.

I think we tend to be braver and meaner over the phone and this is obviously not a good thing. The same is true of e-mail, except here, we can easily turn into a monster. Our note starts with civility, and our first few paragraphs may even reflect maturity and respect, but watch out.

We get all fired up pleading our case to a screen and get angrier and meaner with each word. By the time we get to the last few sentences, you would think the email is from Wolf Man.

Whatever convenience is gained by using e-mail or telephone isn't worth the trouble you are putting into play.

11: Your Lawyer's Place or Mine?

In many divorce cases, the parties and their attorneys will agree to meet in one of the lawyer's offices to discuss the possibility of an out-of-court settlement. This type of meeting is referred to as a "four-way conference."

Four-ways are used in both the adversarial and collaborative processes, but this discussion pertains only to the settlement meetings that take place during traditional or adversarial cases – the cases where the parties are preparing to go to trial. This paragraph does not apply to the four-way meetings taking place in the collaborative law process because the behavior of its participants is automatically regulated by the workings of the collaborative process itself.

The four-way meetings in the adversarial system are optional; there is no requirement to have them. The attorneys agree to arrange for such a meeting only if they feel the parties are capable of discussing the issues constructively. The first meeting usually takes place in the lawyer's office, which is the most convenient or suitable for all four participants. They may alternate offices if there is more than one meeting.

Four-ways can make or break a divorce, and I would be remiss if I didn't mention a word or two of caution. My concern for your negotiation wellbeing is based on what I have observed in hundreds and hundreds of these meetings.

Your spouse is likely to use the four-way as a sounding board for his or her grievances. Since they really have no immediate intention of changing *their* mind, they will not use the conference room as a place to confer. They'll use it as an arena for getting you to change *your* mind.

Be forewarned to walk on eggs because your spouse is sure to get your goat. They'll say and do things that would infuriate anyone, and then expect you to say yes to the deal they want.

Never bite the hand that negotiates with you.

You will be tempted to let loose. Don't do it. You're there to profit financially and mouthing off is bad for business.

With this being said, please understand that a four-way conference is still a good thing. Whenever your spouse travels cross-town to sit in a lawyer's office to discuss settlement with you, it's a good thing. Treat it as such. See it as an opportunity to help your problem. There is no downside to a four-way if you keep your cool and refrain from blowing up any settlement bridges.

As in all conversations with your spouse, walk in the door with the three components of the buddy system approach tattooed to your brain:

1. Avoid aggravating your spouse.

2. Listen to what your spouse says and convince them you heard every word they said.

3. Know what to say and when to say it. Then say it nicely.

And, always remember, if you treat someone lousy, they'll say no.

We're almost there.

We're almost finished with the nuts and bolts of what it takes to have a sensible divorce. We've become familiar with all of the fundamental negotiation and persuasion insights. We understand the three fundamentals that come into play – perspective, emotions, and language/listening.

Finally, we've prepared for the various problems areas on our laundry list of obstacles, specific situations, and curveballs. Now it's time to bring it home.

Now it's time to take a results-oriented look at those last-minute trip wires that can blow things up at the very moment you think you're finally done.

Chapter 12
Where Do I Sign?

You or your spouse has made the initial offer. You have used the techniques in this book to make or deal with a counteroffer. Yet you are still not in agreement.

How do you close the deal?

The Golden Bridge

You don't retreat to your corner and hope your spouse will magically come around. Help break the logjam.

If you and your partner are stuck, discuss the fact that you are stuck. Mentioning the lack of progress without being judgmental or assessing blame is surprisingly productive. Keep your comments very light and indicate your willingness to help resolve the deadlock.

Also, ask yourself –

Would I accept my offer, if I was in their position?
If not, what would it take for me to do so?

It is essential that you retain a certain level of flexibility. This is why it is so important to begin the negotiations by asking for moderately more than you are reasonably willing to accept. Flexibility gives you room to allow your spouse to "win" something that is not really at your expense.

A good part of any kind of negotiations is ego-driven, and divorce negotiations are no exception. Always remember that everyone has to bring home a trophy.

If your spouse's ego is getting in the way, make sure they don't have to pay too great a mental price for backing down later in the negotiations. Build them a "golden bridge" to retreat across and make it known that the bridge will always be open.

You do this by using the standard of the law as a means of helping your spouse to retreat. It is much easier for them to save face by agreeing to follow a law than it is for them simply to give in to you. Following a law is not a sign of weakness, and it allows them to back down with grace.

However, be careful not to come off sounding like an authority on the facts or the law. Do not presume or convey that your insights are superior. You will only infuriate your spouse. Pretend you know less than they do, because this shows respect, even in disagreement.

True Concessions

Concessions are the language of negotiation. They indicate that you see some legitimacy in your spouse's reasoning. Your spouse needs this. Resistance begins to soften when legitimacy is recognized.

Show gratitude for any concessions made. Acting as though you were entitled to a concession will likely close the door on your receiving future concessions.

Concessions lose their value quickly, so, if you do agree to a concession, be sure to ask for a reciprocal concession immediately. Asking "If I do this for you, what can you do for me?" elevates the worth of the concession you are making.

> **DON'T**, however, make the first concession. Studies indicate that doing so is rarely appreciated and often leads to expectations of further concessions.
>
> **DON'T** ask for a specific concession, because that sounds too confrontational. Instead, say something like, "If I have to give a little in order for you to give a little,

I will do so. I hope you will reciprocate so we can bring this thing to an end. We don't really want to be arguing about this same issue a year from now, do we?"

A good negotiator knows the importance of raising one demand for every one or two concessions made. This tactic reduces the aggregate number of concessions and should encourage your spouse to finish quickly before you throw in any more demands.

Also, experienced negotiators report that the temptation to quit the negotiations is often the greatest just before the other side gives in. Remember this because, when you are feeling the most frustrated, your spouse probably is too. Concessions happen suddenly and without warning. Hang in here, because you are always within a minute of things turning around.

Nibbling

Hooray! A deal has just been reached!

Now, however, while everyone is expressing sighs of relief, one of the parties asks for something extra. That's called "nibbling." Don't do it.

It is usually something minor that stems from a legitimate afterthought or involves something not specifically covered in the agreement. Or, someone suggests a minor, dangling item be thrown into their column to take the sting out of a concession they made earlier.

Going after the very last dollar on the table is risky. Many have found it to be the most expensive dollar in the world.

Watch out for nibbling by the other side once the major items have been locked up. We are very vulnerable when we are sensing the relief that accompanies the reaching of a settlement. We can become euphoric (or at least giddy) at this point in time. Our attitude can get too cooperative. Guard against this natural tendency to suddenly become a tad generous.

If your spouse does try to nibble, respond by asking one of these questions:

- Is this a deal breaker? You will neutralize their nibble without offending them. The question politely makes them admit that it is not a pivotal request, and they will back off.

- I hope we're not going to start renegotiating this thing? I was sure we were done. This makes you appear unaffected by the nibble. The implication is that they are insulting you if they mention it again.

- If they will not let go, then pin them down: Correct me if I am wrong, but didn't we agree to settle if I gave in to you on the [such and such] point? I did give in, didn't I? So, the way I see it, there isn't anything left to discuss, is there?

No One Likes a Lousy Winner

One major thing you can do to persuade your spouse to agree to your settlement position is show appreciation. The human spirit needs approval and validation. So, show appreciation for your spouse's services to the marriage and to the family.

Appreciation is not out of place even after a settlement has been reached. In fact, expressing appreciation after the fact shows sensitivity, respect, and class. It lessens the possibility of your spouse having second thoughts and helps to fortify their belief that they made the right decision. No one wants to think they gave up too much, and a few comforting words can go a long way in preventing this. Remember: no one likes a bad winner.

You may be (almost) divorced, but, in many instances, you may still have to get along with one another after the divorce. So be appreciative. For example, say, "I must admit that, despite our differences, you were always a great homemaker. No one could have done a better job, and I'll always be grateful. Just look at how well the kids are doing. We all have you to thank for that."

What could be a better way to complete a settlement than by being a good winner? From beginning to end, you can't go wrong with the buddy system approach.

Conclusion – Your Divorce Masterpeace

Here's the old way of negotiating a divorce settlement (and please let me go to an extreme to make my point). If we were to boil our century-old method of "persuasion" down to its core, it would sound something like this to our spouse:

> My view counts and yours doesn't.
> I am right, and you are wrong.
> You must listen to me, and I don't have to listen to you.
> My settlement position is reasonable; yours is starting to aggravate me.

How's that for salesmanship?

How could we possibly think this would work? Somehow our "let's fight it out in court" culture must have blinded us on how our message would come across to the other party. It is absurdity to believe that words like these could ever entice our spouse to surrender.

The old way of divorce is focused on going to court. This is what our legal system is all about, and this is why law schools train lawyers as they do.

However, divorce lawyers do not go to law school to learn how to destroy families. The first calling of the legal profession is to help people solve their problems expeditiously and in the best way possible. The lawyers' hands are tied in this respect if the parties arrive in the legal system with all their settlement bridges already burned out.

You Really Didn't Want Blood, Did You?

When I told some non-lawyer friends I was working on this book, more than one asked why I would even mention a "nice approach" when most people want blood, not "nice." They make a good point, and it verifies what I said earlier about how divorce gives us an in-your-face attitude.

I agree that we have all heard how divorcing spouses want blood, but this may not be altogether accurate. It depends on the answers to two simple questions:

- If the people who want blood knew they would bleed just as much as their spouse, do you think they would still want blood?

- Would they still want blood if they knew it would cost them the same as a new BMW?

This is the whole point. Blood isn't cheap. It sucks up your money, your time, and your own blood. Who in their right mind wants to waste these precious things and get nothing in return except for a broken family and a lawyer with a new car?

Today is a new age. Accordingly, it calls for state-of-the-art skills, thoughts, and actions. We must try to develop calm instead of a storm.

The recommendations in this book are not just my opinion. They are proven persuasion techniques which are taught and endorsed by some of the brightest and most experienced negotiators in America.

A nasty divorce case can destroy the spirit of the family. That alone makes the stakes very high indeed. Doing what this book suggests will dramatically increase your odds of achieving a divorce that does not threaten what you hold dear.

And, for those who want to keep their already filed cases friendly, simple, quick, and inexpensive, it may not be too late. These ideas are recommended for any stage of a divorce.

Showing our spouse some human warmth, respect, and genuine understanding is what it takes to stay out of divorce court.

I have worked with just about every variety of divorcing spouse: angry, remorseful, vengeful, and peaceful. You name it. You cannot swim in the waters that I have for forty years and not learn something about people.

My experience has taught me that, *as much as we dislike being nice to our soon-to-be x, we dislike wasting our money more.* This is the basis of the buddy system approach. We can get pretty doggone nice once we realize what it costs to act otherwise.

Our country's best negotiators use the techniques described in this book and, in all my years in practice, I have never heard of a professional negotiator who wound up in a court battle with his or her own spouse. None of my colleagues have either.

By now, you should realize that I am not suggesting that divorcing spouses be docile or like lambs going to slaughter. Actually, I see them more as smiling depositors on the way to the bank.

If you follow the simple suggestions I've made throughout this book, you'll have a decent chance of being a smiling depositor, too.

Goodbye, Divorce Wars…Hello, Dotted Line

I know all about human nature and how divorce can bring out the cobra in the best of us. Human nature is not going to change, but our willingness to subsidize its folly might.

The way things are going, one of two things must happen: either people stop getting divorced or they find a way to get divorced without using litigation.

The first isn't happening, and the second is the subject of this book.

Here are four reasons why things have got to change and change quickly:

1. The public is fed up. The "I'm going to be my own attorney" sentiment is expected to become more prevalent. However, not all spouses can or should do their own divorces – even if they are friendly

– and none should ever do their own if the case is contested or if an imbalance of power or knowledge exists between the partners.

2. Lawyers' operating expenses and fees are not expected to decrease anytime soon – unless their landlords and employees cut their rates. (As if.)

3. The number of divorces filed each year shows no sign of declining significantly.

4. No one wants to spend big bucks on a divorce. Many parties are now spending more on their divorce than they did on their wedding, and this just doesn't sit too well with most people.

This doesn't leave us many options. The only answer lies in our finding a better way to divorce. I believe in the buddy system's anti-war approach, and so do those who have tried it.

Of course, this solution is not for everyone or for every case. However, it is an excellent answer for reasonable spouses who hope to stay above the fray.

I am a licensed attorney in Illinois and can give advice only on Illinois law. However, I am permitted to be your long-distance negotiation coach or divorce mediator, no matter where you live. Your mail is always welcome at rk@DivorceBuddySystem.com.

Tomorrow? Who knows? The difficult spouses will have to wait for some future form of dispute-resolution relief to come along. Until then, they will take your place in the line that is waiting to get into the courthouse.

Today, divorcing spouses have two choices: swallow a tough pill or spend a big buck. All things considered, I believe reasonable ones will swallow the pill. If you've read this far, you know there is a better way.

I rest my case.

Index

A
Absolute truths, 13
Adversarial, 11–12
Adversarial culture, 6
Aggression, 93–95
Agreement, 8
Anger, 55–56
Anti-war approach, 117–118
Anxiety, 55, 61–62
Aspect of divorce, 5
Assistance, 9
Attitudes. *see also* Emotions
   discussion with spouse, 6
   right vs. wrong, 43–44
   settlement, 14, 26, 39, 57, 105
   spouse's vs. our, 7, 113, 116
   and trust, 97
Attorney. *see* Lawyers

B
Ballpark number in negotiation, 102
Behavior toward spouse, 27, 41–44
Big decisions, 85–87
Blame, 5, 56–57, 89–91
Body language, 80–81, 107–108
Brain, 3
Buddy system
   and change, 28–30
   control the encounter, 57–58
   Do's and Don'ts, 47–48, 64–66
   eleventh commandment, 25–26, 35, 41–44
   financial cost, 117
   fundamentals of, xii–xiii, 35, 38–39, 109–110
   future changes, 117–118
   and house rules, 44–46
   major requirements of, 27
   miracle words, 58–59
   non-adversarial, non-confrontational, 16
   out-of-session behavior, 21–22
   persuasion, 36
   and settlement, 16, 22
   and settlement process, 46–47
   three second rule, 73
Bullies, 106–107
Buttinsky Factor, 5

C
Carnegie, Dale, 62
Change and buddy system, 28–30
Civil court system, 11–12
Civil trial, 11
Clients
   guidance from expert, xii
   mediator, 20
   settlement discussions, 20
   universal sayings, xi, 16
   vengeance and retribution, xi
Climate of cooperation, 86–87
Collaborative law, 19–21
Collaborative lawyers, 21
Communication. *see also* Language/listening
   language critical elements, 67
   non-confrontational, 62, 68
   via e-mail/telephone, 107–108
Communication skills, 4, 5, 69–71, 72, 73
Compassion, 63, 65–66
Concessions, 112–113
Conflict, 95–97
Constitution, 12
Control the encounter, 57–58
Conventional wisdom, 100–101
Coolidge, Calvin, 67
Coping tool, 3
Court
   approach, 23

constitution, 12
   vs. court-less approach, 23
   and emotions, 15, 20
   lawyers, 115–116
   pain/expense of fighting, xi
   relevant facts and applicable laws, 14–15, 93
   resolution models, 19
   and settlement, 12, 19, 41
Court battle, 26, 61
Courthouse door, 41
Court-less approach, 22

D

Dealing with differences, 53–54
Defensive mode, 7
Discussion with spouse, 4, 6, 85
Disraeli, Benjamin, 71
Divorce papers, 91
Do's and Don'ts
   aggravation, 39
   aggression, 94–95
   attitudes, 93
   basic behavior, 42
   buddy system, 47–48
   concessions, 112–113
   cooperative climate, 87
   emotions, 88–89
   first offer, 100–102
   language/listening, 64–66, 74–76
   minimum rage, 59–61
   perspectives, 53

E

Ear for an ear, 78
Eleventh commandment, 25–26, 35, 41–44
Emotions
   aspect of divorce, 5
   aspect of marriage breakup, 3, 5, 15
   control the encounter, 57–58
   cost of divorce, 116
   and court, 20
   feelings, 87

full court stress, 61–62
house rule, 46
and mediators, 20
minimum rage, 59–61
miracle words, 58–59
negative, 55–56
negotiation fundamental, 35, 48, 54, 81, 110
no place in courtroom, 15
peace academy, 64–66
peace by peace, 63
post-romantic stress, 61
spirits of spouse, 13
talking about feelings, 87–89
Empathy, 63
Expense of marriage breakup, 7–8
Experts, xii, 20, 21

F

Facts of marriage breakup, 8
Feelings, 87–89
Fees, 52
Female vs. male logic, 95–97
Fighting, 5
Financial cost, 30, 117
Financial future, 6, 85–86
First offer, 99–102
Flexibility, 111–112
Four-way conference, 108–110
Franklin, Benjamin, 11, 55
Friendly persuasion, 74–77
Frustration with legal system, 16
Full court stress, 61–62
Fundamentals of buddy system, xii–xiii, 35, 38–39, 109–110
Future changes, 117–118

G

Generous offer and settlement, 86
Golden bridge, 111–112

H

Haggling, 102–103. *see also* Negotiation
Health professionals, licensed, 20

Hearing aids, 78–81
Hear-say, 77–78
Homemade settlement attempts, 7
House rules, 44–46, 71
Hugo, Victor, 29

I
In-session behavior, 22
Irritable Spouse Syndrome, 36–37

J
Judge, 14–15, 23, 26, 61, 93. *see also* Court; Lawyers; Legal system

K
Knock three times, 73–74
Knowledge speaks/wisdom listens, 76–77

L
Language/listening
  critical elements, 67
  Do's and Don'ts, 74–76
  an ear for an ear, 78
  friendly persuasion, 74–77
  he hears me, she hears me not, 71–72
  he said, she said, 69
  hearing aids, 78–81
  hear-say, 77–78
  I'm all ears, 72
  knock three times, 73–74
  knowledge speaks/wisdom listens, 76–77
  miracle words, 58–59
  negotiation fundamental, 35, 46
  non-friction diction, 68
  paraphrasing, 78
  peace academy, 64–66
  settlement, 67, 78
  speakers of the house, 69–71
  as the word turns, 67
Lawyers
  and court, 115–116
  an difficult player, 38
  and divorce papers, 91
  and fees, 52, 118
  mediators, 20
  and negotiation, 108–110
  settlement device, 41
  testifying at trial, 14
Legal system
  adversarial culture, 6
  and assistance, 9
  blame, 5
  civil trial, 11
  collaborative law, 19, 20–21
  court approach, 23
  and courthouse door, 41
  divorce papers, 91
  frustration with, 16
  involvement of, 12
  litigation, 12–13, 15, 19
  mediation, 19, 20
  seeking revenge, 92–93
  spouse and day in court, 14–15
Lincoln, Abraham, 36
Listen to spouse's position, 8–9, 46, 71–72
Listening skills, 76–77, 78–81
Litigation, 12–13, 14, 15, 19
Long-distance coach, 118
Loss, 61

M
Male vs. female logic, 95–97
Marriage breakup
  absolute truths, 13
  aggression, 93–95
  anti-war approach, 117–118
  and big decisions, 85–87
  and blame, 56–57, 89–91
  and conflict, 95–97
  court vs. court-less approach, 23
  court-less approach, 22
  defensive mode, 7
  divorce papers, 91

Do's and Don'ts, 42, 53, 59–61
emotional aspect of, 3, 5, 15
emotional cost of divorce, 116
expense of, 7–8
facts of, 8
feelings, 87–89
income or asset amounts, 6
in-session behavior, 22
involvement of legal system, 12
lack of trust, 97–98
litigation, 14
and loss, 61
motivation for, 83–85
negative emotions, 55–56
negotiation, 7, 36
negotiation technique, 25
and nitroglycerin, 22
and saving money, 30
seeking revenge, 92–93
and settlement, 4, 6, 15, 21, 38, 46–47
settlement discussion, 72
silence the golden rule, 31
spouse's assurances, 3–4
unresolved feelings, 87
and the victim, 92–93
Mediation, 19, 20
Minimum rage, 59–61
Miracle words, 58–59
Motivation for marriage breakup, 83–85

N

Negative emotions, 55–56
Negotiation
ballpark number, 102
bullies, 106–107
climate, 86–87
climate of cooperation, 86–87
concessions, 112–113
financial future, 85–86
first offer, 99–102
the golden bridge, 111–112
haggling, 102–103
at lawyer's offices, 108–110
long-distance coach, 118
marriage breakup, 7, 36
nibbling, 113–114
process, 101
pushing for an answer, 104–105
and salesmanship, 115–116
and settlement, 106, 109, 115–116
showing appreciation, 114
speaking first, 103
spouse heads for door, 105–106
and threats, 104
and trust, 97–98
the ultimatum, 103–104
via e-mail/telephone, 107–108
Negotiation fundamental
emotions, 35, 48, 54, 81, 110
language/listening, 35, 46
perspectives, 35
Negotiation technique, 4, 25
Nibbling, 113–114
Nitroglycerin, 22, 69
Non-adversarial, non-confrontational, 16
Non-confrontational approaches, 36, 62, 68
Non-divorce circumstances, 73–74
Non-friction diction, 68

O

Out-of-court settlement, 26, 108
Out-of-session behavior, 21–22

P

Pain/expense of fighting, xi
Peace academy, 64–66
Peace by peace, 63
Perspectives, 35, 49–54
Persuasion, 36, 97, 115
Post-romantic stress, 61
Power of perspectives, 49–50
Problem-solving techniques, 22
Pushing for an answer, 104–105

R
Reasonable spouse, 37–38
Resolution models, 19

S
Salesmanship, 115–116
Schopenhauer, Arthur, 29
Settlement
   agreement, 8
   attitudes, 14, 26, 39, 57, 105
   and buddy system, 16, 22
   collaborative lawyers, 21
   communication skills, 72, 73
   and compassion, 65
   and the court, 12, 19
   and courthouse door, 41
   discussion with spouse, 4, 6, 85
   and generous offer, 86
   and haggling, 102
   homemade attempts, 7
   and house rules, 45, 46
   Irritable Spouse Syndrome, 36
   language and listening, 67, 78
   and legal system, 92
   mediation, 20
   monetary, xii
   and motivated spouse, 84
   and negotiation, 106, 109, 115–116
   and nibbling, 113
   out-of-court, 108
   and perspectives, 52, 54
   and persuasion, 97
   proposal, 7
   and showing appreciation, 114
   and spouse's behavior, 94
   and the unexpected, 35
   unresolved feelings, 87
   and viewpoint, 71
Settlement discussions
   clients, 20
   court, 12, 41
   marriage breakup, 4, 6, 15, 21, 38, 46–47, 72
   with spouse, 6, 7

Settlement process, 46–47
Showing appreciation, 114
Silence the golden rule, 31
Speakers of the house, 69–71
Speaking first, 103
Spouse
   aggression of, 93–95
   assurances of, 3–4
   attitude, 7, 30–31, 43–44
   behavior and settlement, 94
   behavior toward, 27, 41–44
   and blame, 56–57, 89–91
   communication skills, 4, 5, 69–71
   and compassion, 63
   and day in court, 14–15
   feelings, 87–89
   fighting, 5
   financial future, 85–86
   he hears me, she hears me not, 71–72
   he said, she said, 69
   heads for door, 105–106
   house rule, 71
   I'm all ears, 72
   influence partner's thinking, 4
   Irritable Spouse Syndrome, 36–37
   lack of trust, 97–98
   listen to their position, 8–9, 46, 71–72
   and listening skills, 76–77, 78–81
   negotiation climate, 86–87
   negotiation process, 101
   nitroglycerin, 69
   non-confrontational approaches, 36
   out-of-court settlement, 26
   and paraphrasing, 78
   and perspectives, 49–54
   reasonable spouse, 37–38
   settlement discussion with, 6, 7
   showing appreciation, 114
   spirits of, 13
   and state of mind, 47–48
Sympathy, 63

T

Talking about feelings, 87–89
Threats, 104
Three second rule, 73
Tone of voice, 71
Training for experts, 20
Trial, 12
Trust, lack of, 97–98

U

Ultimatum, 103–104
Understanding, 79–80
Universal sayings, xi, 16
Unresolved feelings, 87

V

Vengeance and retribution, xi
Victim, 92–93
Voltaire, 13

W

Will, George F., 30
Wilson, Woodrow, 28
Word grenades, 89
Word turns, 67

X

Xenocrates, 30

About the Author

J. Richard Kulerski is a veteran divorce lawyer with forty-plus years of courtroom experience. He practices in Oak Brook, Illinois (eighteen miles west of downtown Chicago) and is a staunch advocate of the non-court approach to divorce.

He is a Harvard Law-trained mediator and settlement negotiator, published author, speaker, and divorce negotiation coach.

Education and Training
- Juris Doctor, DePaul University Law School, Chicago, IL, 1963
- Undergraduate at Benedictine College (Kansas) and Loyola University (Chicago)
- Admission to Illinois Bar, 1963
- Admitted to practice in the United States District Court for the Northern District of Illinois, 1963
- Duly admitted and qualified as an attorney and counselor of the Supreme Court of the United States of America, Washington, D.C., August 26, 1971
- Harvard Law School, Cambridge, Massachusetts, Program of Instruction for Lawyers – Advanced Mediation Training (Robert Mnookin, Gary Friedman, Jack Himmelstein, instructors), 2000 (Harvard Law ranked number one in dispute resolution by *US News and World*, 2002)

♦ Illinois State Bar Association Fred Lane Trial Technique Institute, 1996-1997
♦ Harvard Law School Program of Instruction for Lawyers – Program on Negotiation (Roger Fisher, instructor), 1999
♦ George Williams College of Aurora University School of Social Work, Williams Bay, WI – Conflict Resolution and Divorce Mediation Institute (additional training in divorce mediation and screening for impairments), 1999
♦ Pepperdine University School of Law, Malibu, California – Straus Institute for Dispute Resolution, Advanced Family Mediation Skills, 2000 (Pepperdine Law ranked number one in dispute resolution by *US News & World Report,* 2003)
♦ Collaborative Law Training, Collaborative Law Institute, Bloomington, Minnesota (Stuart Webb, instructor), 2002
♦ Pepperdine University School of Law – Straus Institute for Dispute Resolution, Collaborative Law Training, 2002
♦ Thirty-hour mediation externship in Kane County, Illinois, divorce court (in addition to ten hours of extern group roundtable discussion), sponsored through the George Williams College of Aurora University School of Social Work – Conflict Resolution and Divorce Mediation Institute, 1999–2000
♦ Harvard Law School, Program of Instruction for Lawyers – Advanced Negotiation Training (Douglas Stone, Bruce Patton, Sheila Heen, instructors), 2001
♦ DuPage County Bar Association Matrimonial Trial Advocacy Workshop, 2000
♦ JDS Mediation Training Institute, Chicago, Illinois, 1998

Memberships and Distinctions (Past and Present)
♦ Advanced Practitioner Member – Family Section – Association for Conflict Resolution (ACR)
♦ Fellow – Collaborative Law Institute of Illinois
♦ Member – International Academy of Collaborative Professionals
♦ Member – The Mediation Council of Illinois – Board of Directors Member (2000-2001)
♦ Published author – Bar Association articles on collaborative divorce law and mediation

♦ Section Member – Family Law Section of the Illinois State Bar Association
♦ Section Member – Alternative Dispute Resolution Section of the Illinois State Bar Association
♦ Sustaining Member – DuPage County (Illinois) Bar Association
♦ Member – Family Law and Practice Committee, DuPage County (Illinois) Bar Association
♦ Panel Member – DuPage County (Illinois) Bar Association Lawyer Referral Service
♦ Attorney Member – American Responsible Divorce Network
♦ Member – Chicago Bar Association Matrimonial Law Committee
♦ Member – American Bar Association Section of Family Law
♦ Member – American Bar Association Section on Alternative Dispute Resolution
♦ Member – Alternative Dispute Resolution Committee, DuPage County (Illinois) Bar Association
♦ Member – Association of Attorney-Mediators
♦ Member – Family Law Committee, Southwest Bar Association of Cook County, Illinois
♦ Member – Domestic Relations Panel of the Lawyer Referral Service of the Chicago Bar Association
♦ Member – Family Law Committee, Will County (Illinois) Bar Association
♦ Member – National Registry of Who's Who registered at The Library of Congress, Washington, D.C.
♦ Court Appointee – Attorney for the Child or Guardian Ad Litem
♦ Court Certified Mediator – and Appointee, DuPage County, Illinois
♦ Member – Family Law Attorney National Referral List, Institute for Certified Divorce Planners (ICDP)
♦ Peer-Recommended Professional – Divorce Magazine
♦ Founding Associate – Federal Mediation and Litigation Associates (FMALA), Washington, D.C.

Printed in the United States
137220LV00003BA/2/P